A Good Man

A Prisoner of War's True Account of Betrayal and Survival During the Second World War

by
Jeanie Quirt Brown

One Printers Way
Altona, MB R0G 0B0
Canada

www.friesenpress.com

Copyright © 2023 by Jeanie Quirt Brown
First Edition — 2023

The central text of this book is the actual writings of my father, Lorne Shetler, in the form of his diaries, interviews, letters home and prisoner of war logbook. It relays his real experiences and perceptions. If there are any historical or technical inaccuracies, they are not intentional. As narrator, I have drawn on my own experiences as his daughter to draw the various pieces together.

Most images included are family pictures and documents preserved by my grandmother. A few are from unidentified sources, found in my father's personal papers. Others are taken from the public domain.

All rights reserved.

No part of this publication may be reproduced in any form, or by any means, electronic or mechanical, including photocopying, recording, or any information browsing, storage, or retrieval system, without permission in writing from FriesenPress.

ISBN
978-1-03-915719-4 (Hardcover)
978-1-03-915718-7 (Paperback)
978-1-03-915720-0 (eBook)

1. BIOGRAPHY & AUTOBIOGRAPHY, PERSONAL MEMOIRS

Distributed to the trade by The Ingram Book Company

*This book is dedicated to the memories of Lorne and Ruth Shetler:
Always loved, forever missed.*

We will remember...
Jeanie Quine Brown

Table of Contents

Preface	vii
CHAPTER ONE Kingston, Ontario August 2005	1
CHAPTER TWO Napanee, Ontario 1917–1927	5
CHAPTER THREE Napanee 1927–1941	11
CHAPTER FOUR Kingston September 2005	13
CHAPTER FIVE Enlistment 1942	17
CHAPTER SIX Deployment January–June 1943	25
CHAPTER SEVEN United Kingdom June–December 1943	33
CHAPTER EIGHT United Kingdom January–May 1944	47
CHAPTER NINE Mission to Aachen May 24, 1944	55
CHAPTER TEN Tilburg, Netherlands May 25, 1944	59
CHAPTER ELEVEN Belgium June 1944	63
CHAPTER TWELVE Kingston September 2005	69
CHAPTER THIRTEEN Napanee Summer 1944	73
CHAPTER FOURTEEN Germany Summer 1944	79
CHAPTER FIFTEEN The Long March January 2–February 8, 1945	85
CHAPTER SIXTEEN Luckenwalde, Germany Winter 1945	95
CHAPTER SEVENTEEN Luckenwalde Spring 1945	105

CHAPTER EIGHTEEN Luckenwalde Late April 1945	109
CHAPTER NINETEEN Liberation May 1945	115
CHAPTER TWENTY Repatriation May–July 1945	121
CHAPTER TWENTY-ONE Letters from California Summer 1945	131
CHAPTER TWENTY-TWO Letters from Holland Summer 1945	135
CHAPTER TWENTY-THREE It's a Small World	143
CHAPTER TWENTY-FOUR Napanee 1946–2005	145
CHAPTER TWENTY-FIVE To Everything There Is a Season September 2005	155
Acknowledgements	157
Appendix	159

Preface

This is a story about my dad, Lorne Shetler, and a life well lived. A life that was punctuated by the Second World War and his capture by the Germans. A life that later centred on his wife, Ruth, and the four daughters that he raised with her. It may not be one hundred percent accurate in every detail, but I don't apologize for that. I have done my best to transcribe his handwritten notes, his prisoner of war (POW) log, and letters preserved by my grandmother. She kept all his letters, as well as telegrams from the Red Cross and Royal Canadian Air Force (RCAF) personnel, pressed between the pages of one of his accounting textbooks. Over time, those letters fused to the pages of the text, so I have recorded what I can read without destroying the originals. I am sure Grandma Shetler never realized the gift she was giving her grandchildren and great grandchildren, and generations to come, by preserving these personal mementos.

Wherever possible, the story is in Dad's own words. As such, the reader may find some of the terminology is no longer appropriate. It reflects the time in which it was written and is not meant to offend.

I remember my dad returning from a funeral visitation in the town of Napanee, where he was born, raised his family and lived out his life. With a tear in his eye, he said of his friend, "He was a good man." Then he added, "I just hope when I go, someone will say the same of me."

Lorne Melvin Shetler was a good man. One of the best. I record these memories so the generations that follow will know that he and many others like him are responsible for the freedom they enjoy today. Each man and woman who served had their own story. This is my dad's.

I owe a huge debt of gratitude to historian Michael Moores LeBlanc, with whom I connected by chance through an old high-school friend. He has shared his wealth of research and knowledge about the men of Squadron 429 and the Dutch and Belgian Underground. Michael suggested I put Dad's papers into chronological order and that has led to this account. Had we not corresponded, I would not have been spurred to write this.

CHAPTER ONE
Kingston, Ontario
August 2005

Lorne, age 88, sits in the sterile waiting room on the third floor of Armstrong Wing at Kingston General Hospital. It has that unmistakable hospital smell, and the chairs are hard and uncomfortable for someone with arthritis and an old lower back injury. He sighs heavily, and his youngest daughter, who has transported him here, asks, "You ok, Dad?"

With a bit of a scowl and a hint of a snarl in his voice, he answers, "What am I doing here?" She patiently, and a little patronizingly, responds, "We are here to see your rheumatologist, remember?" Lorne does remember; he still has all his faculties, regardless of what the dismissive staff at the care home may believe. She has missed the point of his question. "That's not what I meant," he retorts. "I only ever wanted that when my time came, I would be in my garden, planting or weeding. But you kids and your mother were always harping on me to be careful and told me it wasn't good for me. You just couldn't let me be."

He sees the look of embarrassment cross Jeanie's face, and it is not lost on him that she was, just for a minute, questioning his competence. He feels a touch of remorse too, as he recognizes that he has hurt her feelings. It seems that he says the wrong thing too often these days. The world is changing, and he must watch every word that comes out of his mouth or risk offending someone.

He knows she is trying to help, and he can't, or no longer wants to, deal with the everyday details of life. He is grateful that someone else has taken over the responsibility of banking, paying bills, consulting with the doctors, and bringing him supplies (meaning beer and rum) for his own solitary happy hour. *I have earned that small pleasure*, he thinks. After moving to the retirement home, he and Ruth had fallen into the habit of sharing a beer before lunch was served. With her gone, it does not hold the same appeal. Even the traditional rum and coke before dinner doesn't taste the same. But he looks forward to visits with his brother Gordie or his friend George, and at least he will have a cold beer to offer them. And maybe drink a whole one himself.

His four daughters visit, but those visits are short as they are always busy. They rarely stay for a drink with him because they have to drive. Lynne is on her own now that her husband, Bruce, has passed. Jeanie is working and has a long drive home to her husband, Nick, and their dog. Barb and Carol and their husbands live farther away so can't come as often, and of course there is really no place for them to stay now that the family home has been sold.

The girls think he should move to a smaller room now, closer to the dining room. But he and Ruth were only able to bring a couple of things from their house into the room they shared; if he goes to a smaller room, will there be anything left that is his? Ruth's empty bed is a sad reminder, but the night she passed, his grandson Brad came and slept there so he wouldn't be alone. Maybe if he stays in this room, other family could come and stay too. He doesn't want to move but fears the choice will not be his to make.

He never thought for a moment that a time would come when his daughters would be telling him what to do and making the decisions. When did this reversal of roles take place? He was always the provider, never dependent on anyone else, and his decisions went largely unchallenged when it came to his family. But it doesn't matter now. Let someone else do it if they want; he is tired and he has earned a rest.

So now here Lorne sits, uncomfortable, sad, lost in his memories, missing his wife of 59 years who passed a few weeks ago. She had always been petite, but this spring she began to lose weight quickly and no longer showed any interest in food. She became frailer by the day, and though the doctor didn't express concern, it was obvious something was wrong. By summer, when she began to complain of constant pain, there was nothing that could be done to help. It would have been too hard on her to undergo testing or invasive procedures. No firm diagnosis could be given, but cancer was suspected. He always thought that being three years older, he would go first. He misses her so. He hopes—no, he knows—he will not be in this world much longer. And he is ready.

He finds the past is intruding more and more on his thoughts these days. The long-ago memories that he has chosen to suppress for so many years are now his constant companions. He finds it frustrating that as those memories surface now, he feels a tear make its way down his cheek. He has never been an emotional man. He attempts a chuckle to cover his embarrassment, as though he is just sharing an amusing anecdote from the war. But the tears are real. Tears for the many friends he lost to war. Tears of sadness, frustration, and a touch of guilt, as he wonders why he made it home safely when so many others came back a shadow of their former selves, or not at all.

He has never taken a day for granted since. He is thankful for the life he has been given and the family he cherishes. Too many of his buddies never had that opportunity, and he has tried to live his life in a way that pays them honour.

He thinks back to his early days growing up on a small farm outside the town of Napanee, Ontario, and wonders just where the years have gone.

CHAPTER TWO
Napanee, Ontario
1917–1927

From Lorne's handwritten diary:

I was born in 1917 on a farm just back of Bath, with Dr. Northmore of Odessa in attendance. The fourth of eight kids, Helen, Harold, Bob (older), and Victor, Hazel, Gordon and Ralph (younger), all in order.

The Shetler siblings in 1923. From left to right: Gordon, Hazel, Victor, Lorne, Robert, Harold, and Helen. Ralph was not yet born.

Mother and Dad both started out teaching public school. In those days you didn't go very high yourself, and there was a so-called "normal school" in Napanee that you attended briefly. This was down by Richard Street, off Bridge Street, and I think was part of the old Westward school.

Mother started teaching, I believe at Roblin, real close to her home, and Dad got a job teaching at Denbigh. In those days there was a stage[1] running there and it took two days. I understand the overnight stop was south of Kaladar. To teach school at Denbigh, which was a German settlement, you had to have a knowledge of German and be able to lick the biggest boy in the school. Some of the boys were pretty big because logging was the main industry, and they took part in logging and log drives down the river and attended some school in the off seasons.

I believe they only taught school the one year before getting married and starting farming near Bath, with a plough and a team of horses and not much else.

My first recollection was living out the Newburgh Road on the farm just the other side of Minks Bridge. I don't think I had started school yet when one night, just at dusk, we kids were playing down at the swamp behind the house and the big brick house caught fire. There was an awful commotion and the neighbours came on the gallop. They got some stuff out of the house but of course it burned to the ground.

Fred Henderson, who lived down the road nearer town, over a mile away, had a tenant house that was vacant so we moved in there. Jessie Henderson was teaching at the crossroad school between the Newburgh and Palace Roads, and most of the time we walked there, about two miles.

It wasn't that long before, with some help, Dad had the present kitchen part built and we were able to move back. The main floor had the kitchen and pantry, and everybody slept in the loft over the kitchen. Later on, the rest of the house was added, with a furnace for heat and four bedrooms which became needed as more family came along.

---

1   A four-wheeled stagecoach that offered transportation for paying passengers.

I think the two-holer outhouse burned also, and I remember at some time or other a three-holer was built. Grandpa Shetler came to visit and would sit there and grunt and you could hear him across the yard. We hit it with stones a few times and he threatened to kill us.

They built a big cistern under the kitchen with a cistern pump. After they built the addition to the house, Dad partitioned off a corner of the loft over the sink and got a tin bathtub and ran a drainpipe down to the sink. They heated water on the cookstove reservoir and on the top of the stove and carried it up in pails. We didn't have toothbrushes or toothpaste or too many combs, but at least we smelt a little better. Mother got a pair of clippers and though she wasn't an accomplished barber, she used to cut all our hair and it kept us from getting lousy.

Shortly after I started school my tonsils went bad and they took me to KGH[2] and had them removed, and I was back home for supper the same day. Dad had bought a 1923 model McLaughlin-Buick, a big old touring car that had a light top and side curtains that fastened on with domes. At that time Roblin Hill had no rock cut, and with a gravity fuel feed the only way the Model T Fords could go up was backwards. Our car had a fuel pump on it, so we could roll right up.

Later the hill was blasted out and the stone all hauled away with men and horses. In 1928 this car was traded to Harry Vanluven for a piano. Mother played a little and Helen took piano lessons with Mrs. Scott.

The Newburgh Road was a county road and I can remember when they improved the road. Long before it was paved, they had a toll gate just the other side of the side road. There was a man there collecting toll and I think it was only five or ten cents. In the winter when the side road filled up with snow and you couldn't get a horse and sleigh through it, they made holes in the fences and used the fields. If it was terribly bad, Dad took us [to school] on the sleighs.

There were a lot of kids going there when I started school and the teacher mixed them up, putting a small kid with an older one. When I finished public school there were only eight going there. In the winter it was so cold that we gathered round the box stove. We had a Miss

---

2   Kingston General Hospital. Kingston, Ontario, was the nearest city to the farm.

Luther for a teacher, and one morning Jack VanKoughnet was chasing her around the stove with the poker. Wilbert Hart was bigger and older, and he took it away from him.

Lorne with his classmates at the one-room schoolhouse on Palace Road, Napanee. From left to right: Bob Colter, Bob Shetler, Harold Shetler, Jack VanKoughnet, Jim VanKoughnet, Edison Ungar, Victor Shetler, and Lorne Shetler. Photo courtesy of Ralph VanKoughnet.

Money was awfully scarce, and mother baked bread once a week. She made 11 big round loaves, and it normally got pretty dry by the end of the week. She made all our lunches in honey pails. She dyed flour bags a dull blue colour and made us pants and shirts, and we went barefooted to school in the summer.

Bob wasn't interested in school and quit with Grade 8. Miss Sexsmith told him a few times he might as well be home. One day she told him that, he grabbed his dinner pail and ran out the door. She chased after him down the road. Harry Pringle stopped him and she apologized, but she was right.

When the boys were small, we had a hired man, Harry Herrington, who had been gassed in the First World War. He loaded his Scotch wife and two kids in the back of his old Ford car and went to Niagara. After the war, I stayed there in harvest time at his excellent fruit farm.

A Good Man

The Department of Agriculture was bringing in people from Britain. One day we got an Irishman. We had corn on the cob, which he had never seen. He finished his first cob and handed it back to Mother and asked for some more peas on his stick. We had cherries for dessert that hadn't been pitted. He pushed back his chair and spit the pits on the floor. That finished him.

After that we had a real good English fellow from Yorkshire, and he stayed quite a while (Jack Moffatt).

We had to go to Sunday school, but the rest of the day was ours. We played pond hockey whenever there was ice or we could flood a rink on the river. We had old used skates, but I finally got a new Christmas pair ($2.99). Some of our hockey sticks were made from the woodpile.

In the summer we had a shallow swimming hole and a deep one with a diving board. Mother learned to swim with two cedar blocks with a belt across them.[3] We played softball and often had boys from Strathcona and Napanee. We played tag around the high beams in the barn and it's a wonder someone wasn't killed.

If the gang wasn't too big in the winter, we played cards or crokinole.

When he was fairly small, Gordon got scarlet fever and the house was quarantined. He had to stay in bed for some time. We used to go in and help him eat his fruit and luckily no one else got it. A doctor came in to fumigate the house and the kids. We were lined up on one side of the kitchen table. Bob ducked under the table and the doctor never missed him.

I was wrestling with Bob in the ditch and broke my collarbone and stayed in bed for some time till it healed.

One day Bob was chopping kindling wood and cut a finger off except for a piece of skin. Mother stuck it on and bandaged it up, blood and all. Our hired man took him to Dr. Hall with the horse and buggy. He said to leave it the way it was and it grew back on.

---

3   The children were not given the floats; they were just tossed off the bridge into the creek and told to swim. They all learned quickly.

CHAPTER THREE
Napanee
1927–1941

From Lorne's handwritten diary:

I passed the entrance into high school when I was ten, and I was a little country boy and didn't know what Latin, algebra, etc., were all about. I spent two years in Grade 9 and after that it was easy. I wasn't happy about wearing knee pants when all the boys wore long trousers.

I rode a bike to school summer and winter, roads permitting. Once in a while I got a ride or hitchhiked. When the road was slick with ice, I would skate to school and walk home (three miles).

A bus service started up from Yarker (five cents a day) and the younger kids rode the bus. Nickels were awfully scarce.

When I came out of high school at age 16, I had the offer to go through for a teacher, but I was too young and immature in my own opinion. I worked for Mills Hatchery with chickens for one spring and helped out on the farm. I spent a summer pulling weeds for Don Hawley in his root patch—good pay for the times, a dollar a day and your dinner. Gibbard's[4] were starting boys from school at 12 cents an hour and after a while 14 or 16 cents per hour.

Miles Vine lived in the MacPherson house and worked for Marklin Miles, a local farmer. We knew that some people around the area were getting jobs in the mines at Sudbury. Miles and I went up on the train

---

4   Gibbard Furniture, located in Napanee, was Canada's oldest furniture factory.

with little money and got a boarding house. It turned out that you only got a job if you knew somebody, and there were lines a block long every morning.

There was an ad in the paper for taking pictures and we tried that. We received 95 cents commission for a 9 x 12 picture. I sold some in Sudbury and Copper Cliff, but Miles didn't do well and hung out around a pool room.

There was no future there, so I decided to go home. I got a ride (two dollars) with an apple truck to St. Lawrence Market in Toronto and then took the train home. Miles stayed another week or two and then put his clothes in a bundle and caught a freight home with the other hoboes. He was a dirty, sooty, hungry mess.

Dad bought a rundown, government repossessed farm on the Palace Road. We built a mile or so of fence and a new barn. The idea was that my brother Victor would take it over.

I bought a 1929 DeSoto car with rotten tires with money that Grandpa Shetler had left me, and used it for going back and forth to do the ploughing, etc. Beyond buying a little gas, I still didn't have any money either. The second war had started, but they weren't taking people off farms unless they wanted to go. In the winter of 1941, Victor and I were driving a horse and cutter three miles a day and cutting cord wood for H.C. Empey and doing chores at home in the bargain. We were making about $1.50 a day and it was hard work pulling a cross-cut saw.

Our neighbour Roy Armstrong, later a colonel in wartime, lived next to Minks Bridge and was in the army reserve at the Napanee armouries (now the site of our post office). He talked me into going to summer camp with the local regiment. Harry Babcock was the head, and while some called it the Frontenac regiment, I always called it the Babcock regiment. It was no problem for me drill-wise, etc., as we had cadet drill and inspection every year in high school. Anyway, I didn't go on with it, but while I was enrolled, I helped line the Kingston streets when the Queen visited there in 1939. I went to Kingston and back by train. With that background and knowing the right people, I probably could have joined the army and promptly taken an officer's training course at Brockville instead of joining the air force.

CHAPTER FOUR
Kingston
September 2005

Lorne eases from the wheelchair and shifts his aching body into the mechanical lift chair, a recent "gift" from the government, and settles back with a bit of a groan. Veterans Affairs has been good to him, he must admit. Before the discovery of his aneurysm, when he and Ruth were still living in their Simcoe Street home, they had provided someone to look after the lawns and shovel snow. They wouldn't go as far as paying for gardening, and he had been forced to downsize the vegetable garden by half, but he could still get out there and putter around. After he'd planted and weeded that same little patch for over 50 years, no self-respecting weed would raise its ugly head anyway.

He actually enjoyed when the fellows from Veterans Affairs or their support workers came by. He and Ruth did not venture far by that point and did not have a lot of company, so those visits had given him a new audience for some of the stories he liked to tell. Ruth would usually give him that look that said, *Here we go again,* and then retire back to her knitting or reading with a slight shake of her head.

The kids were all busy but would visit when they could, and he especially loved when the grandkids were there. It just made the house seem less lonely and quiet. Of course, their visits had become less frequent once they were all grown up, off to university or out on their own. He was proud of all of them and thought they had turned out just fine.

And then the inevitable process of aging began to take its toll. He had become less mobile with age and advancing rheumatism, until one day in the fall of 2003, at the age of 86, he could not get out of bed. Ruth called an ambulance. That day was a turning point in his life, as he never returned home again.

Arriving at the hospital at 6:00 the next morning, Jeanie learned that Lorne had an aortic aneurysm and that a rupture may be imminent. The family gathered around him, fearing the worst. When the doctors were able to review Lorne's medical records, it turned out the aneurysm had been there for years, although Lorne didn't recall having ever been told about it. But the doctor said they should prepare themselves, as they might not have him for much longer.

It was a bit of a false alarm as it happily turned out, since that was more than two years ago now. But after being hospitalized for a week, Lorne's muscles were weaker, and his lung function continued to decrease due to chronic obstructive pulmonary disease. The powers that be told him he must go to a care facility.

Ruth hadn't needed care just yet; although she was legally blind, she could manage just fine in Lorne's opinion. But after 57 years together, living separately was not even a topic for discussion. They moved into the care home together, and Ruth actually seemed relieved. They gave the car to their eldest grandson, and the kids sold the house and its contents. Ruth wanted to know who kept what, but Lorne accepted the fact that it was all just stuff and it no longer mattered.

He is now in a wheelchair and on oxygen, which limits what he can do on his own. Veterans Affairs has supplied the wheelchair and the lift chair and increased his monthly pension, but it's not something he can get too excited about. After a lifetime of hard work and saving, he has nowhere to spend the money anyway. He thinks back to when he did not have the time or money to travel; now he has both, but not his health. And so it goes.

With Ruth gone, he hates being here. He used to jokingly say that any day he looked in the paper and didn't see his name in the obituaries was a good day. But that doesn't seem quite so humorous anymore, and there are few good days. Last week Jeanie came for a morning visit and was surprised to find him sitting lost in thought, the TV screen blank. "Thought you'd be watching *The Price is Right*, Dad," she said. He had to admit that he could no longer really see the show, nor hear it very well.

So today they visited her optometrist, who confirmed he has very little sight left due to macular degeneration. It cannot be improved. His daughter is upset, but he knows he will not be here for long, and for the time he has left, he is content to be lost in his thoughts. Before she leaves, he asks her again, as he has been doing for months, "Could you take me to your place at the lake?" He wants to see their black dog, the new hunting cabin, and the view from the deck out over the water. Also, he has requested some fried fish and maybe his favourite raspberry pie, both of which the staff at the home say are bad for him. Mealtime at the home holds no appeal, always bland and flavourless. "Soon," Jeanie says, but she has been saying that for a while, and he knows it needs to be very soon.

CHAPTER FIVE
Enlistment
1942

Canada had joined the Second World War in September 1939, and by 1941, though they weren't conscripting farmers, Lorne began to toy with the idea of signing up. They wanted recruits with at least a Grade 12 or 13 education, which he had, and he took the notion that he would like to fly, deciding that if he could get into the air force, he just might enlist. Lorne went to the recruitment centre, and they told him to come back in the new year.

In the intervening months, the family weighed in on his decision to enlist. His dad said little, but Lorne could read in his expression that he thought it was a foolish idea. His five brothers teased him endlessly about going off to be a hero and win the girls, but deep-down Lorne knew they respected his choice and maybe even wondered if they should go too. It seemed glamorous and exciting. His sisters, Helen and Hazel, with whom he was very close, voiced their concerns and tried talking him out of his plan, but it never seemed like their whole hearts were in that effort; they too thought going off to war was romantic.

With his mother, he avoided talking about the possibility of going overseas. He knew she was worried, and when he looked in her eyes it was the one time that he experienced some hesitation.

Lorne had been seeing Ruth Boston, a pretty redhead, for a while now. She chummed around a bit with his sister Hazel, who was the same age, and they often attended the same dances, picnics and social events around town. Ruth had grown up the youngest of four siblings, on a farm just south of Napanee in an area known as Hawley's Woods. Her brother Leslie had also enlisted. Apart from his family, he would miss Ruth most, and he was quite sure the feeling was mutual.

Lorne had no overriding feeling that he must enlist for his country or that it was somehow a noble thing to do. He was bored. There weren't any good work prospects at home, and flying sounded like fun.

So, in January 1942, he signed up. They gave him a train ticket to Ottawa, where he had a medical, and he was on another train to the Manning Depot at the Toronto exhibition grounds that same night.

***

From Lorne's handwritten recollections:

There must have been 2,000 men there in the sheep pen, etc. [of the exhibition grounds]. I was confined to barracks for two weeks for shots, uniform, etc. After maybe a month or more, I was sent to Trenton[5] for guard duty for several months. Trenton was Canada's number one flying station. There were a lot of us, so we each only did very little guard duty on the towers with a search light. They had old World War One rifles and a clip of five shells that you weren't supposed to fire. One guy shot a rabbit one night and caught hell for it.

We had quite good instructors there who taught us Morse code, navigation, etc., and had plenty of drill.

Initially the airmen just straggled across the road to the flying side, and then they put in gates. The gates weren't liked but anyway some of us were conscripted to work for the service police [SP]. They gave us a revolver but no shells! They said that the gun was just for show and that we couldn't hit anything if we tried, and they were right.

Posted from there to Eglinton Hunt Club in Toronto. Number one initial training school, a lot of classes, PT [physical training], and drill.

---

5   Canadian Forces Base Trenton was the hub of the British Commonwealth Air Training Plan during the Second World War. It was also a short distance from Lorne's hometown of Napanee.

A Good Man

The first day we were out on the square by the street and our drill sergeant said, "This is the best section of Toronto, and you SOBs better act accordingly or else."

With the classes from Trenton, I could have passed right away.

I developed great big ugly carbuncles[6] on my legs and they put me in the hospital for a while. They didn't hurt but they looked like hell until they broke. I was excused all physical training and drill and that broke my heart. Also put in time on the Link Trainer.[7]

Sent out to Oshawa for pilot training on Tiger Moths. Had quite a lot of ground school but little flying. That was a hazy, hot summer and there was no horizon for learning to fly. I got just ten hours in over two months. Anyway, they said I was too slow so I had a washout check with the commanding officer. This was a civilian school with an instructor on loan from the RCAF. My instructor had two [men] from our course; the other guy was American and already a flyer. They sent 70 of us there and told us when we went that 35 had to wash out. I was cheesed off but didn't shed any tears.

Eddy Thompson (football player for the RCAF team) took me up and said, "You're safe enough but you're already finished." He said, "I'll give you some satisfaction," and so I soloed after I washed out.

Four of us [washed out] at the same time: Darryl Gourley from Saskatchewan, Mac McKay from Nova Scotia and I can't remember who the other guy was. Washout school was at Trenton and with the Commonwealth air training scheme[8] there was a surplus of men waiting for re-muster and posting. In the mornings we went for a walk back of the airport, sat on the rail fence, shot the bull and smoked.

In the afternoon they always had a movie on. There was no hitch-hiking allowed, but I knew the SPs from working with them and they would get me a ride to Trenton or Belleville.

---

6   A cluster of boils.

7   A flight simulator used for key pilot training in the Second World War.

8   The British Commonwealth Air Training Plan was a joint effort of the United Kingdom, Canada, Australia and New Zealand to train Allied air crews in Canada, taking advantage of the country's ample open space and its distance from the front lines.

I got a ride home [to Napanee] one day, and since there wasn't much traffic, I started looking for a ride back at 6:30 in front of Tierney's funeral home. There were already two guys waiting there. Sam Delver, a preacher from back of Belleville who was going with Marion Hawley from Morven, came along and said if I was still there at midnight, he would give me a ride. Another guy joined us and Sam gave us a ride to Trenton.

The four of us [who washed out] all re-mustered to bomb aimers. After about two months a posting came to bombing and gunnery schools in Alberta, Saskatchewan and Manitoba. They told us we could take a choice or wait for one to the east. Since Darryl Gourley's people had a wheat farm at Watson, ten miles from Dafoe [Saskatchewan], we went there. They had old Ansons, Bolingbrokes and Fairey Battles from the First World War. The weather turned so cold that the only planes that could fly were in the hangars.

Lorne with a Fairey Battle bomber used for training at the RCAF station in Dafoe, Saskatchewan.

A Good Man

Every second weekend, a special train took the whole station to Saskatoon except the SPs. They had an obstacle course there, but we complained that we couldn't keep clean and we won the argument. We had been issued new uniforms and used them for flying. We got the parachute stock from the shops and a little guy brought in a dose of crabs and all in that end of the 'H' hut got them. Every morning the bunch of us were paraded to sick bay. As each one went in behind a screen, a nice friendly redheaded nurse handed us blue ointment and red barn paint. As each one came out, she would say, "How are they this morning?"

After winning the argument regarding our uniforms, we were confined to barracks at the station and couldn't go to Saskatoon. What they didn't know was that Darryl's brother brought the car in with lots of tractor gas and we went to dances anywhere within 50 miles. Lots of polkas.

I had some bad teeth, abscessing, and got them pulled. They said, "You're going to Malton from here and you can get a partial [denture] plate there."

We got down to H1 navigator's school at Malton and learned map reading, etc., around the country. We had more aircraft recognition training, etc. We got one "B" wing[9] and the RAF [Royal Air Force] got their laid on 6% commissions; the Canadians got none.[10] Our record of disobedience from Dafoe followed us. The main course got embarkation leave but for four of us; we got leave (two weeks) but were posted to Lake Erie B & G[11] to practice bombing moving targets (ships towed). The lake froze over so they sent us to Manitoba for so-called high-level bombing, 28 officers and four non-commissioned officers [NCOs]. We were the first NCOs to go on that course. When we finished, we got another leave.

---

9   This references his Bomb Aimer Wing, earned upon graduation.

10 Lorne implies there was to be an increase in pay after graduation, but that it was only given to the RAF and not the RCAF airmen.

11 Bombing and Gunnery School.

A newspaper clipping from the January 28, 1943 *Kingston Whig Standard*, saved by Lorne's mother Ethel.

An undated photo of Lorne in his RCAF uniform during training.

CHAPTER SIX
Deployment
January–June 1943

While Lorne was finishing up his initial training, the war was still raging in Europe. A meeting of Allied leaders was held in Casablanca, French Morocco, in January 1943, including British Prime Minister Winston Churchill and US President Franklin D. Roosevelt. The outcome of the Casablanca Conference was a unified decision to launch a joint bomber offensive on Germany and make it known to the Axis powers that the Allies would accept nothing less than unconditional surrender from Germany, Italy and Japan.

February saw Guadalcanal[12] taken by American forces, effectively ending Japanese expansion plans. That same month, Hitler's previously advancing armies saw one of their first significant defeats at Stalingrad, and by the end of February, Mussolini had fallen. It appeared that the Allied strategy was making a difference.

But for Lorne, the war was just beginning.

***

---

12 The Guadalcanal campaign in the Solomon Islands was the Allies' first major land offensive against Japan.

Royal Canadian Air Force
Halifax, N.S.

March 26, 1943

Dear Mother:
I'm not doing much this afternoon so thought I'd better drop you another line even though I haven't heard from you yet. I have had two or three letters forwarded here from Paulson. I was talking to Johnny Martin, P/O, at noon and he was telling me about two more of the boys from his bunch who are out there now taking the High Level [bombing] course.

Have finished up here drawing out our webbing[13] *and been in the compression chamber and got everything finished. I couldn't stand the pressure at 35,000 ft. so I guess I won't be going up that high. I haven't done much the last few days except just put in the time.*

I've been down in Halifax quite a lot and gone to a couple shows. They have such long lineups in front of them that it's hardly worth waiting. Three of us were out last night with some sub-lieutenant nursing sisters from the navy hospital here. One of them was a cousin of one of the boys and she had some friends. The one I was with was from Charlottetown. We're supposed, as far as we know now, to see them tomorrow night.

How is the weather there? If it's anything like it is here, the boys must be trapping by now. There's no snow here at all and if it weren't for the damp breeze from the ocean it would be really nice. I've got to buy up a little more stuff yet but hardly know what more to get except maybe some toilet paper. They say they haven't any over there at all, so I don't know just what they do use.

I told Gordon Shetler in Montreal that I might get down to Sydney to see Harry while I was here, but I guess I won't be able to make it. I enquired where Sydney was and they told me it was just four hundred miles away so maybe it's just as well.

How is everybody coming along? I didn't bother writing to any of the family except Hazel. We're not allowed to say anything anyway and I guess

---

13 Lorne seems to be referring to the issue of a web kit, which was made of dyed cotton webbing and consisted of a waist belt, braces, and various pouches for carrying survival essentials.

everything is censored, so I guess I might as well close for now. Hope everybody is well.

Love to all,
Lorne

***

Late March 1943

Standing next to his bunk, Lorne checks his suitcase one more time. He has little to pack in the brown cardboard suitcase: a few changes of socks and underwear, soap, toothbrush, razor, some extra toilet paper and a couple of pencils. He adds a deck of cards that he purchased yesterday in case he can round up a card game. Uniforms, a great coat, and boots will be provided, so just a couple of changes of civvies should do, he thinks. He has tucked away in the corner of his case a picture of the family and one of the pretty redhead he has been seeing. He has promised Ruth that he will write, and he wonders if he will get any letters from her. He hopes so. He has no clue how long he will be gone or if he will even make it back home, but if he does, Ruth Boston is someone he could see himself settling down with.

Tomorrow at this time he should be on his way to England. Some days he finds it hard to remember his life on the farm. So much has changed since he left Napanee. He hasn't even made it overseas yet, but he has already seen more of the world than he ever imagined he would. He has been out west and now east and has met lads from all over Canada. He is excited, but if he is honest with himself, he is also a little anxious. He has never been on a ship, and he wonders what it will be like. He says a silent prayer that he won't be seasick in front of the guys.

***

From Lorne's handwritten diary:

We finally got on the Queen Elizabeth, 18,000 aboard. We zigzagged across the Atlantic (six days) and landed at Greenock on the Clyde and then train south to Bournemouth (a holiday centre). March weather in Halifax but spring in England.

Had a short leave and posted to the Orkney Islands—tip of Scotland. Officers travel first class and NCOs travel tourist (third class). We were there for two weeks flying the main fleet and had a conducted tour of "Alabama," a US battleship. One day supposed to take pictures with an air camera. I had a good mark in photography from Malton but they had no cameras and I didn't know one end from the other.

Posted to the Isle of Man (Irish Sea) for an intensive ship recognition course: all ships and flags of the world.

***

RCAF Overseas

April 24, 1943

Dear Mother:
Received your very welcome mail for the first time today; had a letter from you, Helen, and Hazel. Have been wondering how you've all been coming along but didn't expect to hear any sooner. I sent the cable on a Monday so it didn't do too badly.

I just got back today from seven days leave. I spent a couple of days in London and the rest in Kent just outside of London with Mrs. Thackeray of Bexley Heath.[14] *I saw most of the sights of London, Buckingham Palace, Westminster Abbey, St. Paul's, Marble Arch and all the other sights... Expect to be posted right away to an AOS*[15] *for further training along the same line as we took at Paulson so I guess I'll be where I was looking for, on Coastal Command some time or other. Hope the weather is nice too on the Isle of Man. Just three of us are going and the rest may remain here for quite some time.... Where we are going they say nothing is rationed so that should help out a lot....*

Love to all,
Lorne

---

14 Although I am unable to verify, I believe the folks he speaks of visiting in Bexley Heath were residents of the UK who offered to host airmen away from home.

15 Air Operations Support

A Good Man

***

RCAF Overseas

May 10, 1943

Dear Mother:
Just came into London on leave and am dropping a line from there. Am being posted to another training school with a few days in between. It's really some change from the Orkneys to London. We were wearing our great coats before but now it would feel better with our coats off. I bought a coat yesterday and am going around London in civilian clothes, and does it ever feel good. We're spending a few days in London and going out to Bexley Heath to see these people we stayed with before. There are Canadians and Americans wherever you look out here but I still haven't seen anyone I know. I was at RCAF Headquarters yesterday after some cigarettes and got a picture of Jim Moore and will send it along later on. I think I have received all of your letters up until the first of May and one from Hazel and Vera which I'll have to answer later on. I suppose everything is going strong now at home. Coming down on the train I noticed that they are starting over here too. Hope all is well.

Love,
Lorne

***

RCAF Overseas

May 18, 1943

Dear Folks:
Just received your lovely box last night and was really surprised to get anything so soon. I know it's not very much to say, but thanks an awful lot. It's impossible to get most of that stuff over here where I am. One of the boys is in the hospital and when I told him I had some tomato juice and peaches his eyes just about popped. A couple of the boys have had cigarettes from home, but this is the first parcel like that and it's really appreciated.

I'm glad it came when it did, for we expect to get posted very soon. We may get some more leave first, it's hard to say though. Edison Ungar was supposed to write and tell me when he was getting his but I have only heard from him the once. If I do get leave, I guess I'll go to London again even if it is pretty well out of the way. Having some exams right now and am getting some more.

We took some pictures on Saturday and will send some when we get them back. It stopped raining for a few days and it's been just like summer the last few days. Some of the boys have been in swimming and I may go in tomorrow if it's nice. We get the afternoon off for sports and I think I'd sooner go swimming than play cricket. Just been to a variety entertainment show just now put on by some English players and it was very good but they do crack some pretty corny jokes. Some Aussies are here shooting the bull now and I think they do it just about as good as the Americans…

***

RAF Station Skeabrae
Kirkwall, Orkney

June 16, 1943

Dear Mother:
I think I've received most of your letters up until the end of April and the first of May and the one parcel. Thanks very much and Vera and Helen too, though I haven't answered them yet.

I've just finished up my leave and am starting in at my new station. It's nice to be back in England again and this place is set right in a farming and fruit district in the central part. I've only one fault to find so far and that's the way the station is scattered so far apart; I think if I can't get a bicycle I'm going to wear out a lot of boots. I'm still with the Canadian boys but the Australians and the Royal Air Force have been sent to other stations. I'm mostly in with Canadians and when I leave here I should have a pretty good chance of being with a Canadian squadron which will be all right with me….

***

A Good Man

From Lorne's handwritten diary:

Posted to Operational Training and at Honeybourne to fly twin engine Whitleys[16] to patrol in Bay of Biscay after subs. We got crewed up[17] there, pilots, navigators, bomb aimers and wireless operators.

There was a foreign-looking guy with three shoulder flashes, Guatemala, USA, and Canada, pilot and a great studious guy. His navigator asked me if I would like to fly with them. I agreed and made a good choice and also got an RAF wireless operator. We were to be an NCO crew but had to have one officer, Ron Rudd.

***

Lorne's Crew:

Pilot: Mario "Ferdie" Fernandez de Leon, whose father was a surgeon in Guatemala and whose mother lived in San Francisco.

Navigator: Ron Rudd of Owen Sound, Ontario, a flying officer and student at the Ontario Agricultural College in Guelph.

Wireless Operator: Bert Dawson, RAF, from Alkrington, Lancashire, England.

Tail Gunner: Ken Jackson, RAF, from London, England.

Bomb Aimer: Lorne "Air Raid" Shetler of Napanee, Ontario.

The crew later switched to a four-engine Halifax[18] when the Whitleys were discontinued and added more members:

Mid-Upper Gunner: Bob "Jughead" Christie of Toronto, Ontario.

Flight Engineer: William "Mac" Stewart of Manitoba and Vancouver, British Columbia.

---

16   A British bomber aircraft

17   Assigned to a crew

18   The Halifax was a British heavy bomber that entered service in 1940 and played a key role for Bomber Command.

Jug, Mac, Bert and Ken were each newly married: Jug and Mac just prior to going overseas, and Bert and Ken while on operations. The others were single.

Lorne, third from left, atop a bomber with unidentified crewmates.

CHAPTER SEVEN
United Kingdom
June–December 1943

June 28, 1943

Dear Folks:

...My pilot, a boy from Guatemala, and I were into Birmingham for the day Saturday and bought a couple of second-hand bicycles. He paid about $15 and I paid about $20 for mine. This place is spread out a long way and it should save a lot of walking. We haven't done much flying yet, and it's still on the twin engine planes....

Lorne cycling with his crewmates in the spring of 1943. From left to right: Robert Christie, Ronald Rudd, Lorne Shetler, Mac Stewart, Ken Jackson and Bert Dawson.

Jeanie Quirt Brown

***

RCAF Overseas

August 28, 1943

Dear Mother:
Received two letters from you and one from Helen the other day. I had a blue letter and an airgraph written since they were, so there wasn't much new in them. I finally got my leave and am down in London for a while and then going to Edinburgh. It's raining here right now and not very nice for a holiday. I was down to Bexley Heath yesterday but there were two New Zealanders down there so I just called on them. I'm staying at a Canadian YMCA club and it is not too bad. I'm just going out to RCAF Headquarters now and see what they're giving away today if anything. Our crew got a very good recommend from the last station and I was recommended for a commission[19] *if that means anything. We change over to four-engine planes at the next station and that will surely be a big improvement over the last ones. How is everyone coming on; OK, I hope? I'll be dropping another line shortly when I finish my leave.*

Love,
Lorne

***

September 23, 1943

Dear Folks,
…There's really not very much new here to write about, doing a little studying and some flying. This continuous training gets a little monotonous and the sooner we finish the better. The Halifax is a good aircraft and we've got a good crew, five Canadians and two RAF.…

…Daryl Gourley is here right now and we're talking of going somewhere to a show tonight. My pilot and engineer are night flying or Ferdie would probably be going too. Mother, you said something about you hoped he wasn't too young. Well, he's 25 and about the same size as I am so he's

---

19 A promotion to commissioned officer.

not so very small either. The engineer is 36 and comes from Manitoba. He wanted to know where I came from, and he says some people from his district came from around Napanee. He used to be a farmer and is a pretty steady-going kind of fellow....

Love,
Lorne

***

On arrival in the United Kingdom, Lorne had been posted to Scapa Flow, Scotland, and then Isle of Man, before arriving at the Third Operational Training Unit near Stratford-on-Avon where they practiced circuits and bumps, a pilot's term for touchdowns and quick takeoffs. His first actual operations base was Leeming in Yorkshire.

***

From Lorne's diary:

Nine crews stayed at Honeybourne and nine went to Stratford-on-Avon. Another NCO crew (Smith, pilot, and MacGillvray, bomb aimer) stayed there. The pilots, navigator and bomb aimers threw in money for the least bombing errors. Mac at AB[20] and I at Stratford ran neck and neck until a night trip to Wales with 400-pound sand bombs. Somehow or other Mac lost his, so we got the money.

While we were at Stratford, they stopped making the old Whitleys, so that cancelled the subs[21] and we were posted to conversion on four-motored bombers. We were posted to Leeming in October. It was a permanent station before the war and we were quartered in row housing that had been married quarters during peacetime. There were six NCOs in our crew and we shared a house. Downstairs there was a living room and kitchen separated by a wall with a fireplace. Two cots were set up in the living room, and upstairs were two bedrooms, each

---

20 RAF Abbots Bromley

21 Operational training at Honeybourne involved flying Whitleys to patrol the Bay of Biscay after submarines.

with a set of bunkbeds. The upstairs bathroom was supplied with hot water from the pipes in the fireplace. We didn't spend much time there except to sleep as it was generally cool and damp. We were rationed one wash tub of soft coal per week for heat, which was not adequate to dispel the damp, so we occasionally raided the fenced-in coal pile after dark. Still, it was not wise to be caught stealing coal so we didn't have enough heat for daily bathing. Smith's crew, posted the same time as us, were living next door. They were shot down on their first mission and no report.

***

Lorne was now ready for operations. In the months of August and September 1943, there were both continuing atrocities and signs of hope that the end of the war was near. All of Sicily was now controlled by Allied forces, and Portugal allowed the Allies to set up air and naval bases on the Azores Islands. In September, the Italians defected from the coalition of Axis powers and finally surrendered to the Allies.

***

429 Squadron RCAF

November 6, 1943

Dear Mother:
Received your airmail of October 22 a couple of days ago and very glad to hear that you are all OK. Had an airgraph from Hazel and answered her this morning. Letters from home are never censored, are mine? Nice to know that you got your apples and Dad is able to go after them. They are holding a victory loan drive here and I don't know whether I'll get a bond or not.[22]

There's not an awful lot of news here. I got back OK from my three days in London and had a nice time, saw a few shows, went to a theatre, etc., and got rid of what money I had. Ferdie's shoulder is better now and we're starting to do a little flying but still not on operations, but we never know when. The weather

---

22 Victory Loans were Canadian Government appeals for money to finance the war effort.

has been wet, foggy, and generally miserable, but the sun is shining today for a change. Was watching them bomb up the other day and met George White from Napanee; he's a corporal rigger with our squadron. I haven't had a parcel of cigs now for two months and it's too bad, for somebody must be getting them. Very glad to have pipe tobacco and cigars though. Hope you're well, will write more later.

Love,
Lorne

***

November 11, 1943

Dear Mother, Dad, and kids:
Just a line letting you know that I received your Christmas box yesterday. I opened it up but will do as you say and leave it until Christmas. I don't feel right about it when I'm not sending anything home, but thanks a lot anyway. Ferdie was going to add a note but he's not here right now so I guess it'll have to be later on. That parcel really came through in a hurry.

It's quite chilly here today, but for a change the sun has come out. I've heard how miserable it gets here in Yorkshire and I'm starting to believe. The other squadron on the station were given a crest yesterday and had a big party last night. They were sort of adopted by Metro-Goldwin-Mayer pictures and call themselves "The Lion Squadron." Anywhere they go on leave they are supposed to get into an MGM picture for nothing. There was talk of the Calgary Brewing Co. adopting us, but I haven't heard any more of it. They gave us our own aircraft the other day. "R" for Robert. It's not new, been in about ten operations before we got it. We've done some local flying but there's not much doing while the moon is full. Our rear gunner (RAF) has a 72-hour pass this weekend to go to London to get married. Our wireless operator is his best man, and the navigator is going. None of the rest of us are, but we're giving him a pound apiece for a wedding present. That'll be three married men; mid-upper gunner and engineer both got married just before they were moved across...

Love,
Lorne

***

It was clear from Lorne's letters home that he was very happy with his decision to join this particular crew. He was forming a strong bond with a few of the men, especially their pilot, Ferdie. The two spent much of their free time together. The following is an undated letter to Lorne's mom back in Canada.

Dear Mrs. Shetler,
Just a line or two to let you know the other boys and I are taking good care of your little boy. Of course, there are times when he's quite a handful, but somehow we'll manage and bring him home to you soon.

Just,
Ferdie

***

429 Squadron RCAF

November 19, 1943

Dear Mother,
How are you coming along? OK, I hope. Just a line to thank you for the parcel. I've also had one from Helen and one from Vera. I'll have to write them and thank them, perhaps tomorrow. I hadn't expected anything in the world like all that and don't hardly think I deserved it.

Well, we got on our first operation last night over Ludwigshafen. I don't hardly know how we happened to be on it because it is quite heavily defended; I guess the other raid at the same time on Berlin must have had something to do with it. They really had some beautiful fires and it was a pretty good show. Somehow or other when you are over there, you don't think of the poor devils down below. The idea seems to be to get rid of your load and get away as soon as possible. There was quite a lot of heavy flak but thank the Lord we had enough height to be above it. It is a relief though when you cross the enemy coast on the way home. So now we've got 27 more of them to do. I had a letter from Ron Stobs the other day and he has three in on Lancasters. We're just sitting around tonight by the fireplace and going to have something to eat. Mac, our engineer, got some canned meat and we're going to make up some toast… It's been quite nice here the last couple of days, almost too nice for Yorkshire. There's some snow around on all the hills and it freezes a little ice at night but nothing like it probably is around home now. I wish the weather here was like it is at home, though. Well, not an awful lot more for now. Hope you're all well and not working too hard.

Love to all,
Lorne

***

429 Squadron RCAF

November 27, 1943

Dear Folks:
Have just received your nice airgraph of November 12 and was reminded I hadn't written you in a few days. I had a box of cigs from Gordie, sent October 1, the first box in around three months. I haven't bought many English smokes and have got along pretty well. I had a box of chocolates from Helen and smokes from the Rotary Club. Thanks to you all and I'll drop a line later on. Between the bunch of us we do pretty well, and even the ground crew, all Canadians, bring stuff over to our hut to eat. One of the boys got either seven- or ten-pound parcels (I forget which) all in a heap. They're a good bunch of boys and really keep our kite, R for Robert, in good shape.

So, you've had some snow but I'll bet it's a lot nicer than it is here. We've had some soft snow but it's terribly foggy here right now. I hope it stays that way for a couple days so they can't put us on the night we go on leave. It's Saturday night now and if it stays this way, we may get away early on Monday instead of Tuesday. Mac and Bob, the engineer and mid-upper gunner, are going to Edinburgh, and Ferdie and I are going to Leeds and then London. Ferdie wants to see his embassy and I want to see Pay and Accounts. My F/Sgt[23] dates back to July and I still haven't had any money

---

23 Flight Sergeant designation, a senior non-commissioned rank

for it. We like the station better than we did when we first came here. We've landed at two or three other stations and when we see what they're like we feel more satisfied. A bunch of boys from a Lancaster station are here right now and I asked them how they liked our mess. It sort of shook me when they said how much better it was than theirs at their station. I've run into quite a few of the boys I used to know and they tell me one of the boys I was with at Initial Training School in Toronto has finished a tour of operations in the Middle East already. I guess we're kind of slow but none of us are in any particular hurry. Gus White gave me four of his latest Napanee Beavers[24] *the other day. He has a subscription and they send them straight over to him. Ferdie and I were to see "Mademoiselle France" at the show just now and Bob Christie, our mid-upper gunner from Toronto, Jughead we call him, has just gone to a dance at the YMCA. It's pretty miserable out though and I'd just as soon be here by the fireplace. There was a stand down this afternoon and I got paid and played a few billiards. Well, I guess that's about all for now. I'm running out of room. I hope you're all well and not working too hard.*

Love to all,
Lorne

***

429 Squadron

December 7, 1943

Dear Folks:
Just received your letter of November 8 today when I came back from my leave. I spent a very nice eight days divided between London, Leeds, and Bexley Heath, saw a few shows and went to a couple of dances and generally enjoyed it. Ferdie went with me, except down to see the Thackerays. They're coming along OK and seemed quite pleased to see me. I gave Mrs. Thackeray one of the boxes of chocolates from Christmas and she was very happy because you can't get the like over here at all.

---

24 The Napanee local newspaper

I had a box of nuts from Hazel today and then just before going on leave had Helen's chocolates and Gordie's cigs. I'll have to write them a letter and thank them. Mac, our engineer, went down to the post office today and got six parcels at once. That boy (37 years old) really gets them, but he is one swell guy.

There's nothing much doing here right now while the moon is so bright. Bomber Command prefers to work in the dark, so until it goes down things will be pretty slow. At the rate we're going we figure we'll finish a tour in about two years and a half. Our ground crew have our plane name now, "Reich Express." They're thinking of putting a picture on it of Hitler down in a toilet hole and a pretty girl flushing the toilet.

So Cameron Shortts is on a Pathfinder squadron;[25] *they have to be good to be on one of them. We're perfectly happy here where we are. The weather is still kind of mixed up here. It was foggy yesterday and last night and tonight it is drizzling. I wish we had weather like home instead of this stuff. There are an awful lot of people in England down with the flu already and it's supposed to be quite an epidemic. We've got our fireplace going here tonight and Ferdie and I are both writing letters, and we're having something to eat later on. What's it like around home now and how is everybody? All right I hope, and not working too hard. Hope you have a Merry Christmas. I'm spending mine on the station and hope to have a good time.*

Love to all,
Lorne

---

25 Pathfinders were elite squadrons of experienced airmen who used flares to mark targets for Bomber Command.

The air and ground crews pose with their new airplane, *The Reich Express*. Lorne is on the bottom left, Robert Christie and Bert Dawson are top left, Ronald Rudd is third from the right and Mac Stewart is on the far right. Pilot Ferdie is in the cockpit.

***

December 22, 1943

Dear Folks:
Just a line to say that everything is okay, even if there's not much news. It's really miserable and cold out this morning. We're on another station right now and won't be able to go home unless it clears up. We're still not doing much flying, only been out once in the last month. As our wireless operator says, "it was a piece of cake." We should have a holiday either over Christmas or New Years. It doesn't seem much like Christmas over here and there is very little you can buy in the stores without coupons. We go on leave again on the fourth of January, just four weeks since our last seven days. They really do pretty well by us with leave.

A Good Man

Thanks a lot for your last parcel, which I got the other day. It was the one with the cookies, cheese, raisins, etc. I had a nice one from the church at the same time. It had, among other things, a pair of mitts knitted by Mrs. Stan Wales. I'll drop a line to the church, but will you tell Mrs. Wales I got her mitts and thank her.

I was in the YMCA hut the other day and ran into one of the McKeown boys from Varty Lake. I didn't know him but he knew me and we had quite a talk. He's a fitter (engine mechanic) and his brother is a few miles away at the last station I was at. I am starting to run into some of the boys that I was with before I washed out. They're just starting to get on squadron now. I guess I moved ahead a little faster than they did.

… Hope you're all well and going strong. Hope you have a Merry Christmas and a Happy New Year.

Love,
Lorne

***

December 26, 1943

Dear Folks:
It's the day after Christmas and believe me, it was 200% better than I expected. It doesn't seem like Christmas out, but more like spring right now. For being on a station, it couldn't have been much better. I was in the officers' mess in the morning, airmen's at noon, and sergeants' mess at night, and ended up at a station dance. I borrowed a tunic from one of our ground crew and ate dinner with them and went to their dance too. They had the same as we did: turkey, roast pork, brussels sprouts, celery, tomato cream soup, apple sauce, dressing, mince pies, Yorkshire pudding, and sauce, milk, beer and cigarettes. You couldn't have asked for any better anywhere. To finish it off I got three parcels the night before Christmas, one from you, one from Ruth Boston, and one from the Palace Road,[26] so it was a real Christmas. I only hope the English people did a quarter as well.

---

26 Brother Victor's farm

About as nice a thing as we got was from one of our ground crew, Carl Paul of Vancouver; a little bound placard hanging here over the fireplace:

"Be thee O Lord, within me to strengthen me, without me to watch me, over me to cover me, under me to hold me up, before me to lead me, behind me to bring me back, round about me, to keep off my enemies on every side."

He couldn't have done any better if he tried....

SERGEANTS' MESS, R.C.A.F. STATION, LEEMING.
CHRISTMAS DINNER 1943.

Menu.

CREAME OF TOMATO SOUP

ROAST TURKEY.   ROAST PORK.
ROAST POTATOES. CREAME POTATOES. BRUSSELS SPROUTS.
APPLE SAUCE.
SAGE AND ONION STUFFING.   BROWN GRAVY.

CHRISTMAS PUDDING.   RUM SAUCE.   MINCE PIES.

CHEESE, BISCUITS AND CELERY.   FRUIT.

CIGARETTES. BEER AND MINERALS.

At this festive season, I wish to extend to every Senior N.C.O. of this Station my heartiest greetings and warmest wishes for great happiness in the New Year.

It is hoped that the coming year will see us re-united with our loved ones, and, we may now have the satisfaction of having seen considerable progress towards that happy day.

To one and all, good luck and good cheer.

B. Bryans, O/C

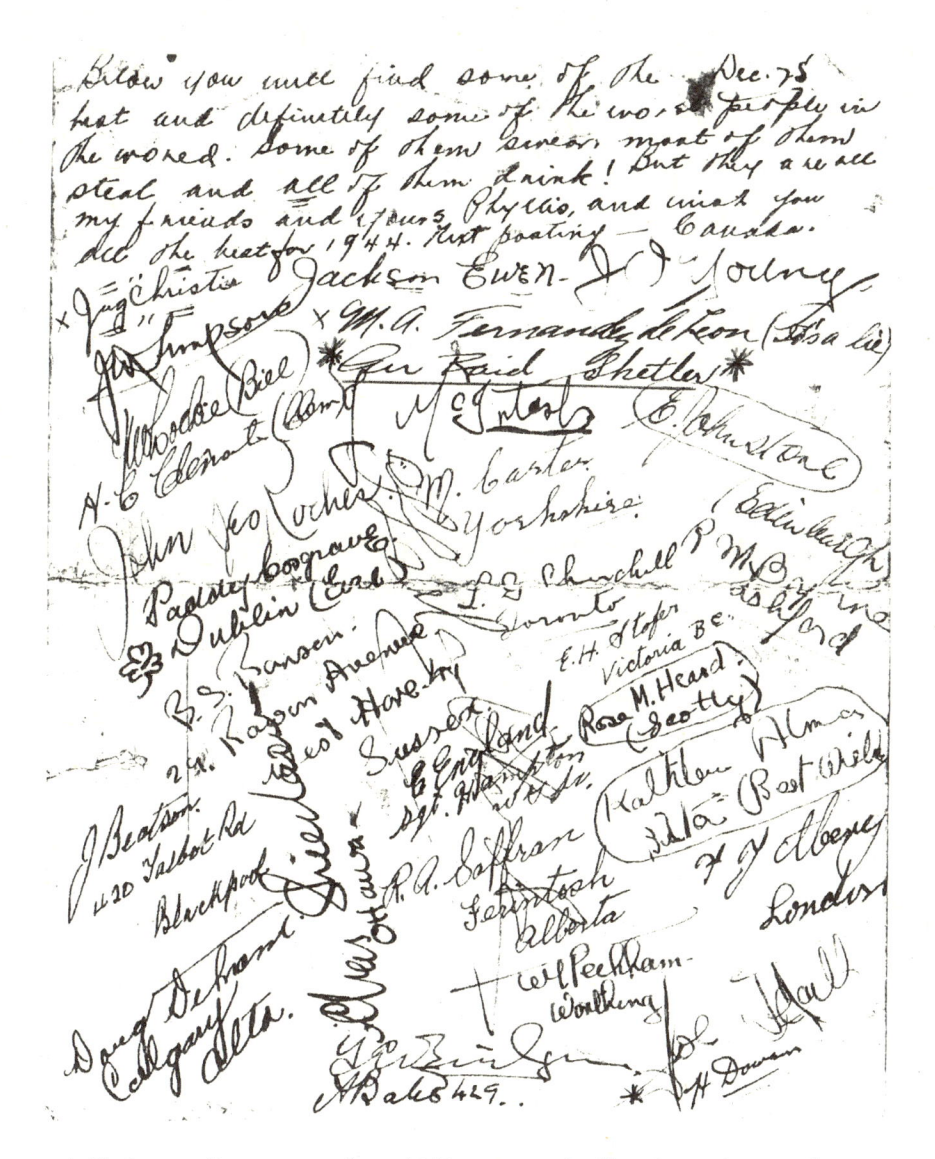

A Christmas dinner menu from 1943, autographed by airmen in attendance; Lorne signed it as "Air Raid Shetler." The menu was given to Michael LeBlanc by Mac Stewart's widow.

CHAPTER EIGHT
United Kingdom
January–May 1944

Undated letter from February 1944:

...Have just received about four letters from you this week and a parcel of food. Thanks a lot for it; it was swell and we really appreciate the canned food. I was mad about the apples, though. They were pretty badly spoiled. We all had a Canadian snow apple at Christmas, and we get oranges in our rations when we fly. By the way, don't worry about me spending coupons on stuff to send home because we don't get any; only the officers get coupons because they have to buy their own clothes.

This is Sunday afternoon and not an awful lot going on. There's some local flying and we should be on it, but Ferdie is not feeling very well. We've got another "R" in place of the old kite we had, but we hope to get a new and later model in the near future. Our crew had our pictures in the Canadian news weekly and I'll send you one as soon as we get them. They were taken at the interrogation after a trip. We haven't done too much lately, but we were over to the "Big City" again the other night. How is the winter coming on over there? Hope it's still not too bad. It's really mild here and just like spring. Some of us are going down to the local church tonight and I don't think we even need our greatcoats...

The crew being debriefed after a bombing mission. Left to right: Ronald Rudd, Mario "Ferdie" Fernandez de Leon, Lorne Shetler, Robert Christie, and an unidentified officer.

***

429 Squadron

February 11, 1944

Dear Folks:
Just got a letter from Dad the other day and one from Mother tonight. Thanks a lot for both of them; I was really surprised to get the letter from Dad… And so you've finally got a little winter too. It snowed hard here the other day for a few minutes and we just sat in the hangar and watched it. It only was a spit and then was gone. It's pretty mild out again tonight.

They're still not working us too hard, not flying very much. By the way, ours is called the "Bison" squadron and we were officially adopted by the CNR[27] about a month ago. We had big shots here and they took pictures

---

27 Canadian National Railway

of the doings. I was on leave at the time and didn't see it, but I've ordered some pictures of it. I sent two or three pictures home the other day and I hope you'll get them sometime later. Thanks a lot for sending Ferdie the shirts, somebody swiped all his…

***

429 Squadron

February 21, 1944

Dear Folks:
Just came back from leave tonight and got your letters of February 6 and 12. I've been going to write for the past week but was waiting until we came back "home." We had a swell leave up in Scotland. I spent a day at the Stobs' in Glasgow and the rest of it at the RAF Club in Edinburgh. The weather was good, and it was hard coming back to Yorkshire again. It is so wet and miserably cold and damp here. We missed three operations while we were on leave and then we came back tonight and they tell us that the squadron will not be operational for the next month or so at least. Our training will go on just the same though. Mrs. Stobs tells me that Ron went missing on a raid on Berlin on January 3 and still no word of him. It usually takes about two months to get word through, and he has a 75% chance of being a POW. I was invited out to their house for supper one night, and on Sunday we went through a Canadian minesweeper[28] from Toronto and I had supper on board. They hadn't been over very long and still had plenty of Canadian grub. We even got a good big can of tomatoes home with us. We could have got more but one of the boys lost the keys to the storeroom overboard.…

…Well, I guess I should get back and look at the fire. We're tired and going to bed early. No need to worry at any time, but the next two months it's training again. Hope you, Dad, and everyone are well and not working too hard.

Love,
Lorne

---

28 A small warship used to remove or detonate mines.

429 Squadron

February 28, 1944

Dear Folks:
…Thanks a lot for the two parcels I got last week. I also got one from Hazel and cigs from Gordie and have written to them. I still have Helen's sleeveless sweater so I gave Mac Stewart, our flight engineer, the one you sent. He wanted to put a note of thanks in this letter but I guess he'll have to do it later. And Ferdie really appreciated the necktie. The other day I sent a few snaps and a Scottish tam for Lorna and hope they get home okay, though it may take some time. We were out three times last week and got one trip for it. Our squadron has been taken off the main targets now so it will make a difference. And the moon period is coming on too. It would be a beautiful day for flying today, though we're not on.…

Love,
Lorne

***

429 Squadron

April 9, 1944

Dear Folks:
I've got two or three letters from you and a box since I came back from leave. Thanks a lot for everything and I don't know how you send so much. I have plenty of everything right now and am doing fine. I also had nuts from Laura Burgess and cigs from Gordie and Victor and Stan and Mrs. Hart, so I think I'm doing pretty well.

It's Easter Sunday and I was to the station church this morning. I was planning to go to the village church tonight, but since then plans have been changed. It's pretty foggy out right now but it's expected to lift. I had a pretty good leave in London, Bexley Heath and Leeds. I was down at Thackerays' for two or three days. Luckily there were no raids while I was down there. Joe Bagnall couldn't meet me because his leave was cancelled at the last minute. I'd have liked to have seen him too.

A promotion came through while I was on leave so I'm now a warrant officer (W/O). No word yet about a commission. I guess they figure I'm too lazy or something. We are getting another new plane, still the same make but it has all the latest navigation equipment, etc., and should be better all around. It'll be "Q for Queenie" now though instead of "R for Robert." We hated to see the other one go, but still have the same ground crew, etc....

***

429 Squadron

April 17, 1944

Dear Folks,
I just got a blue airmail this morning and had one last Tuesday too. Glad to hear that Lorna is coming along so much better. She must have had a pretty close shave. I had a box of Laura Secords[29] from Hazel this morning and another from Ruth Boston, so I'm getting a lot more chocolate and stuff like that than I did when I was home.

There's really no news here at all. We went to France and Belgium over the holiday but it doesn't help very much when you only get credited with a third of an op for those trips. It would take a long time to finish a tour.[30] It's been pretty cloudy and dull around here and not much flying. We may fly this afternoon; I don't know yet. Our new "R" really runs nice and I've only been up in it once though yet. They are doing pretty well by us for new aircraft; this is four now and two of them brand new....

***

---

29 Laura Secord is a Canadian chocolate company.

30 A typical tour was 30 operational flights, not exceeding 200 flying hours.

429 Squadron

May 1, 1944

Dear Mother:
Just yesterday I got your letter of April 21 and also a parcel. Thanks a lot for both of them, they were just swell and arrived in good shape. You asked me what else you could send me. Well, the canned stuff is better than the chocolate bars, and I wonder if you could get some tomato juice. The can of tomatoes is gone already and was a real treat.

I guess you and the men must all be working pretty hard about now. The weather should be pretty nice about now. It's swell here right now but I feel awfully lazy. I think I'll have to look up a place where I can swim one of these days. Yesterday was Sunday and I almost felt homesick lying around here. We were out last night and I just got up a little while ago and had dinner. I hear that we're doing a little flying again tonight but haven't gone down to the hangars yet today.

I had a letter from Helen the other day and also one from Vera but I hope they don't expect an answer too soon. I wrote to Stan Muir at the RAF Club in Edinburgh the other day and told him to look for us up there on leave around the 18th. It seems to be a long while since we came back from London three weeks ago. I guess it must be because we never get a day off. I was going to send flowers for Mother's Day but figured there was no use with all the flowers around home right now. Well, this is all for now. Hope you're all well and not working too hard.

Love,
Lorne

***

From Lorne's diary:

Crew were posted as replacements to Squadron 429 (later designated CNR Bison). Their motto: *Fortunae Nihil*—Nothing to Chance.

We had a few close calls on operations and bombed Berlin a few times, once from 25,000 feet. The longest [operation] we did was a nine-hour trip to Nuremberg in bright moonlight and we lost 96 planes with at least 675 aircrew. Of course, quite a few would have had a chance to bail out and be taken prisoner.

We used to say in the RCAF (and a lot of us still do) that any landing you walk away from is a good one. Our Halifax crew was flying with No.6 Group RCAF bomber crew from Leeming, Yorkshire. Early one morning returning from an op, we forgot to set our altimeter for height above sea level and came in too high.

We thought we were never going to touch down and when we did, we ballooned. We bounced and settled seven or eight times before we finally started to roll. Our RAF rear gunner must have taken an awful pounding in his turret but he came on the intercom with "Hey Skipper, that last landing was pretty good!"

CHAPTER NINE
Mission to Aachen
May 24, 1944

Lorne and crew are briefed as usual for a mission to Aachen on the edge of the Ruhr Valley. Aachen is a central hub for coal and heavy industry where the main rail lines from Germany to France and the Low Countries[31] intersect. They are told they are going in across the town, that rail yards are the target, and to be sure not to overshoot. Fifteen aircraft are ordered for the squadron. Lancasters will be following, which makes this a major initiative. Orders are to bomb at 12,000 feet and then drop down to 6,000 feet on the return over Holland, keeping alert as they fly over an aerodrome where 45 German night fighters have just relocated. They understand, as all Allied air crew do, their role in this mission; the railyards are needed, whatever the cost, and their crew is expendable.

This isn't training anymore; this is real life. It is their 26th mission since the first one on October 21, 1943, always in the dark, each lasting about five hours, plus many shorter flights that did not count as full missions. Their first trip in active combat had been the worst; that red iron being fired up at them at 20,000 feet was pretty scary. The second crew that had gone up with them that October night did not return. If they needed any reminder that this could happen to them too, that had driven it home in a painful way.

---

31 Belgium, the Netherlands, and Luxembourg.

The crew had been given ten days of leave in May 1944. All have returned on the 24th just in time for the Aachen operation to discover their usual plane, the Ruhr Express, had been taken up by another crew who failed to return from their mission. They are flying the wing commander's Halifax III LW-124 this night.

The seven men prepare as they do for each mission and take off from Leeming in aircraft AL-N[32] carrying sixteen 500-pound bombs. Visibility is good, despite clouds and light rain earlier in the day. They lift off at 2256 hours. As the bomb aimer, Lorne is up front in the lower level with the navigator and the wireless operator. The pilot is up higher, along with the flight engineer, and behind them is the mid-upper gunner in his turret, with the rear gunner behind him. On their trip to Aachen, they see several aircraft go down. Each man gives up a prayer of thanks that they have not been hit and another to protect the crews of those planes that have been. There are light winds and light cloud cover as they cross over the east railway yards, and at 17,000 feet they can plainly see their markers. There's no flak[33] to contend with as they carry out their mission.

Bomber Command will later report that the two railway yards were badly damaged. Many bombs fell in the town of Aachen itself as well as in villages close to the railway yards, killing 207 people and seriously injuring 121 more. Nearly 15,000 people were displaced. Many casualties were reported in the nearby villages, and in Eilendorf, near the Roth-Erde yards, 52 were recorded killed.[34]

Another bombing mission completed and it's time to head for home. The plane banks north, descends to 9,000 feet and then heads west at about 220 miles per hour. There is still a lot of activity and

---

32 AL were the letters assigned to the squadron for all their aircraft. Each squadron normally had three "flights" composed of about eight aircraft, though numbers varied. Each of the three flights had its own range of letters (excepting some letters such as "I" that might lead to visual confusion): for example, A,B,C,D,E would be Flight One, J,K,L,M,N would be Flight Two, and R,S,T,V,W would be Flight Three.

33 Anti-aircraft fire

34 *Bomber Command Monthly Review*, May 1944.

they see more aircraft drop from the sky. They spot one in a downward spiral about ten miles south of them, hit by flak is their guess.

And then, at 0120 hours on May 25, their luck runs out. Their kite has been hit. They had not seen any flak and did not know the enemy fighters could fly below them and shoot upward.[35] The plane is in an out-of-control dive from 8,000 feet with the port engine on fire. They are plummeting, everything turned upside down, and they are plastered to the ceiling. Then the skipper, Ferdie, straightens it out and feathers the engines. Over the noise, they hear the order from Ferdie to bail out. They frantically check their parachutes and out the front hatch they go, the cover jettisoned. Ron Rudd, navigator, is first out; Lorne, bomb aimer, is close behind. Time is running out as the wireless operator, Bert Dawson, jumps. It all takes about four seconds but to them it seems like a slow-motion movie. And then the unimaginable happens. The plane, carrying Lorne's four remaining crew mates and best buddies, disappears in a fiery crash. It is 0122 hours. It will not register until later that his mates are gone. Ferdie, Mac, Bob, and Ken.

***

Unknown to Lorne, in the early morning hours of May 25, the Tilburg Fire Brigade attends a fire in a wooded area that has been sparked by the crash of a British aircraft. They discover Ferdie's body in the cockpit and the bodies of the other airmen around the wreckage.

It is later reported that the German night fighters got 15 of 100 Halifax bombers on the way back over Holland, then 15 of 100

---

35 Though the method of shooting upward from below the target aircraft had been developed during the First World War, its tactical use was not fully understood or recognized by the Allies at this point in the Second World War, and many crews were taken by surprise. Being unfamiliar with the tactic, crew that survived usually reported they had been hit by flak rather than fighters. The attacks came from beneath the aircraft, out of the bomb crews' line of vision, so it was virtually impossible to counter the attack with defensive fire. The German Luftwaffe gave this method the name Schraege Musik, roughly translating to Strange Music.

Lancaster bombers an hour later.³⁶ Most all had been victims of two German aircrew in Me 110³⁷ night fighters flown by Heinz-Wolfgang Schnaufer and Karl-Heinz Scherfling. Schnaufer will take credit for the downing of Lorne's aircraft and five or six more the same night.³⁸

Heinz-Wolfgang Schnaufer, pilot of the German Me 110 night fighter that reportedly downed Lorne's plane.

---

36 There were differing reports, as the Bomber Command report of night operations for May 24–25, 1944, states that 18 Halifaxes and 7 Lancasters were lost.

37 Messerschmitt Bf 110s, known as Me 110s, were twin-engine planes used by the Germans for night fighting.

38 Heinz-Wolfgang Schnaufer was born in 1922, five years after Lorne, yet at the tender age of 22 he had established himself as one of the greatest night fighters of the Second World War. Most of his 121 declared victories were against British four-engine planes like the one Lorne's crew was flying. He was awarded Germany's highest military decoration that year.

CHAPTER TEN
Tilburg, Netherlands
May 25, 1944

Lorne came down hard in a second-growth bush, landing in a small tree and then ricocheting off a stump. He wasn't sure if anything was broken but was in a great deal of pain in his buttocks and back. He learned later that he had broken his tailbone and the next disc. After resting there awhile, still in the dark, by and by he began to walk slowly in a southerly direction.

When daylight came, Lorne moved off the road and hid in a farmer's henhouse. Later that same morning, the market farmer, Piet van Meel, discovered him and brought food: raw bacon, bread, and water. Piet did not speak English but tried desperately to explain that he would do his best to find him help. Van Meel was not part of the official resistance. He had two sons in the German SS[39] fighting in Russia, and he could not afford to be caught hiding an Allied airman. He also had neighbours on either side of his home who were believed to be collaborators. Yet he wanted to help this young man.

A short way from the farm in the Delmerweg area of Tilburg, Netherlands, a family by the name of Cornelissen ran a bakery. A friend, Mr. van Rooyen, was staying with them while trying to keep

---

39 The SS, or Schutzstaffel, began as a protection force within the Nazi party, but became one of the most powerful organizations in Nazi Germany. The SS carried out the genocide of millions of Jews and other targeted groups, as well as countless other war crimes and crimes against humanity.

under the radar of the German army. He overheard Lorne speaking English to Piet as they passed. He immediately grasped the danger of the situation, as German troops were, at that very moment, scouring the countryside for survivors after the downing of so many aircraft during the night. He intervened, promising Piet he would take Lorne to one of the few homes he knew to be safe and the people trustworthy.

Janus and Maria Cornelissen were not members of the underground, and they were fully aware of the danger they were taking on, but they could not turn away an airman who had been shot down for his efforts to liberate their homeland. They gave Lorne an old suit of clothes and a pair of boots, disposing of his uniform, and put him to bed. Janus' brother, also named Piet, was a teacher who had studied English for a time and lived in a monastery of the order Frater van Tilburg. Though he was not part of the underground either, he had long suspected that another friar, Ermericus Gemert, was. He approached him cautiously.

By nightfall they had an answer from the monastery. "Don't ask any questions. Take the airman to a streetcorner in Tilburg, give him a bag in his hand, turn around, and don't look back over your shoulder!" And so they did, because doing it any other way could have been a great risk for all involved. They knew nothing of Friar Emericus' underground activities beyond the implication that he was involved. Any such activity in the order was strictly forbidden. To be exposed would be dangerous, not just for him but for all the brothers in the order. Janus never disclosed the exact corner where Lorne was dropped off. He put his trust in underground connections.[40]

Shortly after Lorne left the care of the Cornelissens, German SS troops made an assault on the nearby house of an old widow, Corba Pusins, who was hiding eleven Allied air crew members and their helpers. The Germans came in via the front door and left by the

---

40 Records from the Dutch Archive show that three brothers of the Order of Frater van Tilburg were instrumental in connecting Lorne with the underground: Frater "Piet" Cornelio Petrus (Joseph Maria Cornelissen, Janus Cornelissen's brother), 12/07/1909–14/14/2002; Frater Ermericus (Emericus Van Gestel), 25/11/1913–25/12/1977; and Frater Martiniano (Cornelis Van de Sanden), 22/03/1916–31/03/1945. Frater Martiniano was later arrested by the Germans and sent to Bergen-Belsen concentration camp, where he died.

A Good Man

back, killing every person inside. Janus and Maria were devastated to think that Lorne may have been one of the victims, but no one could confirm or deny. The person who betrayed the widow to the Germans was never found, and even after the war was over, the residents of the town knew it was too dangerous to speculate.

But Lorne had once again been spared. After his clandestine street-corner rendezvous, he had been taken to some row housing where he was given a bed and food and several days to recuperate from his excruciating back injury. The lady of the house was in a late stage of pregnancy and already caring for her husband, who had a broken leg. They had a gun, a radio, and a German living next door!

After the better part of a week, a new contact brought Lorne out to the countryside. As Allied forces stormed the beaches of Normandy on D-Day,[41] he was staying in a covered hole in the woods and being fed by a Dutch farmer.

Two other airmen joined his underground hideout, assisted by a Dutch resistance network known as the Andre Group.[42] Started by Sprang-Capelle Mayor Adrianus Smit and local electrician Jos van Wijlen following the German occupation of the Netherlands in 1940, the local group had quickly expanded to include contacts throughout the Netherlands. Their activities, which began with distributing illegal magazines and countering German propaganda, eventually escalated to sabotage of trains carrying ammunition for the Germans and ships conscripted for German use. The Andre Group was also active in hiding groups of people who feared their fate at the hands of the Germans, including Jews, Dutch soldiers, and those who refused to work for the enemy.

Most importantly to Lorne, they had become involved in assisting the crew of Allied planes shot down over the Netherlands. Andre

---

41 On June 6, 1944, troops from the UK, US, Canada, and France attacked German forces on the coast of northern France in the largest military naval, air and land operation ever attempted. This marked the start of the campaign to liberate Nazi-occupied northwest Europe.

42 The name of this resistance group was chosen as a tribute to one of its young members, Andre Boesman, who died of pneumonia.

Group provided shelter and food and would accompany them to the Belgian border, the first stop in an escape route back to England. In total, the group would be credited with assisting 187 airmen in their escape from the Netherlands.

Andre Group members provided Lorne and his new companions with civilian clothes and Dutch passports and moved them to the farmhouse of Janus Rooyackkers of Moergestel Group, another link in the underground connection. Following the D-Day invasion, however, Germans and their horses were moving into the area. The airmen's stay at the farmhouse ended abruptly when six soldiers who needed to be billeted entered the front door, forcing them to scramble out the back. A Dutch family by the name of Seimons insisted the airmen take their bicycles, and the men pedalled toward the Belgian border about 15 miles away. Lorne would later remark that the family would rather lose their bicycles than their lives for aiding Allied airmen.

Lorne was escorted across the border with air gunner Vernon Joel of 405 squadron and two fellow airmen from 429 Squadron: mid-upper gunner Charles Shierlaw of Ottawa, Ontario, and wireless operator Walter Bush of Westbourne, Bournemouth. Their kite had been shot down the same night as Lorne's at about 0130 hours over Tilburg. Another crash and burn, and one of the many planes claimed by ace Karl-Heinz Scherling that night. The men spoke of their respective crews and wondered about their fates. Shierlaw was confident that Lee Caunt, their navigator, had gotten safely out of their plane, but was resigned to the notion that the other four had not survived the fiery crash.[43]

Charlie, Wally, and Vernon's stories were similar to Lorne's in that they had sustained minor injuries and were helped by Dutch farmers who sheltered and fed them. Now, thanks to their kindness, the four airmen were moving through the channels of the Belgian underground, their lives inextricably linked.

---

43 Deceased were Pilot Flight Lieutenant Thomas "Barney" Rawlinson, Bomb Aimer P/O Arthur John "Art" Murphy, Flight Engineer P/O Albert "Bert" Bates, and Rear Gunner Flight Sergeant James "Red" R. H. Cochrane.

CHAPTER ELEVEN
Belgium
June 1944

What happened to the men once they reached Belgium is the stuff of movies, but unfortunately was all too real.

Lorne and the three other downed airmen, Wally Bush, Charles Shierlaw, and Vernon Joel, had followed their Dutch guide from Andre Group at a distance on their borrowed bicycles. It took about an hour to reach the border, where they hid the bicycles and continued on foot into Belgium.

Wally realized he had lost his dog tags somewhere along the way. Members of the military were issued two dog tags for administrative and record keeping purposes. If an airman was killed, one tag would remain with the body and the other would go back to the base so that person was accounted for. The tags also usually carried a letter designating any religious affiliation, so that if the soldier was left behind, the people responsible for burial would have that information. Rather than leave Wally with no tags, their guide instructed Charlie to give Wally one of his.

Once across the border, they were passed off to a new member of the underground and proceeded the 40 kilometres to Antwerp by train. Fortunately, they did not attract any attention in their hand-me-down civilian clothes, and upon arrival at the station, they boarded a tram for a short ride to a café that was to be the next meeting point.

A man by the code name of Donald, real name René van Muylem, met the four men and escorted them to the apartment of a woman named Yvonne de Ridder. She was about 30 years of age and was very active in the resistance, harbouring Allied airmen and helping them evade capture.

Yvonne de Ridder (circa 1948), the resistance member who hid Lorne in her apartment in Belgium.

A Good Man

René van Muylem, known by the code name Donald.

Donald was surprised to find there were already two RAF chaps staying with her, and the new arrivals made things a bit crowded. She did her best to make them comfortable in the small space, even daring to enlist the help of a downstairs neighbour in the building for sleeping accommodation for Walter, and she made sure the men were fed. There was little to occupy their minds, and they passed time swapping stories and taking turns watching from behind the curtains for any unusual activity in the street. They wondered how long they might be there and when and how they might be smuggled back to England.

A few days later, Yvonne received a message from a contact in the resistance that her identity had been compromised. She was advised to get rid of these airmen and save herself. Harbouring and aiding Allied airmen was a crime punishable by death. When Donald arrived that afternoon and heard the news, he immediately advised that the men should be moved to another hideout, and a plan was hatched.

In her book, *The Quest for Freedom*,[44] Yvonne recounted how the airmen were to be handed off to her contact Donald:

> *"The plan was as follows. Two of the men would walk to the side street, just to the right of our building, then turn right onto that street. If they were not followed, they were to light cigarettes after turning the corner onto the back street, then proceed along that street to the Grande Chaussée, the highway to Brussels, where Donald would be waiting.*
>
> *Once the 'all clear' signal was given by these two, the third was to leave, this time turning left into my avenue as he went out the front garden, and thus straight through the assembled German plainclothes agents, to rejoin the others at the same gathering point.*
>
> *After making sure the men had understood his instructions, Donald left abruptly. Lorne Shetler and Walter Bush chose the first route. Our hearts were pounding. We watched them walking unhindered toward the side street; the time lapse before they reappeared on the side street had seemed long. They kept up their long, steady stride at a normal pace, not hurried. After turning the corner onto the backstreet, they stopped and gave the all-clear signal by lighting cigarettes, then resumed their walk."*

All went well with the first part of the plan, and after seeing Lorne and Walter light their cigarettes, signalling that contact had been made with Donald, Charlie left on his own a few minutes later and met up with the other three a short distance away. They walked about five miles, though it felt much longer, trying to be nonchalant while inwardly they were anything but. When they finally reached their

---

44 Yvonne de Ridder Files, *The Quest for Freedom: Belgian Resistance in World War II*, Fithian Press, Santa Barbara, 1991.

destination, they entered a building and climbed to the fifth floor. There were German soldiers guarding the entrances, and Lorne would wonder in retrospect why that didn't send up alarms for the three men. But at the time they were happy to be on their way home and grateful to the Belgian Resistance for their efficiency in bringing them this far.

They were given all the fine food and drink they could want and enjoyed the company of their new helpers. The mood was light. They were each asked to fill out forms that would ostensibly be used to confirm their identity with the British. Their hosts explained that this was to ensure that no one was posing as an Allied airman in order to infiltrate the underground organization. It was impressed upon them that their lives depended on their candidness and their identity being verified by the Brits. It was later understood that these questionnaires and conversations were valuable sources of intelligence for the Germans regarding the Allied war effort, courtesy of over 180 unwitting Allied airmen who passed through the Antwerp pipeline between March 1944 and the evacuation of the city in September.

That evening they were told they would not be staying the night and would be taken to a new location. They were surprised when they saw the fine German touring car that would be their transport. The three airmen were comfortably seated in the back of the car, and each noted, without commenting to the others, that their car did not even pause at the German roadblock along their route.

When the car finally stopped and the back door was opened by their driver, they were greeted by uniformed German Gestapo. They had been betrayed! Donald wished them better luck next time and went on his way. It had been the men's misfortune to encounter a false line of the resistance, known as the KLM Line, tasked with infiltrating the escape line and facilitating the arrest of Allied airmen. "Donald" had sold them, as he had many airmen before and after, for the paltry sum of 25 pounds each. In Belgian court after the war ended, van Muylem claimed responsibility for the arrest of 157 airmen. He was sentenced to death before a firing squad.

Yvonne was imprisoned for her role in the resistance but avoided execution when Antwerp was liberated. Her father, however, was killed.

The need for secrecy in the underground activities was great. Each person had their role, and the less they knew about their contacts the better. This way, if one person was exposed and interrogated or tortured, they would have little to reveal and the other links in the chain would be protected. However, this also meant that it was difficult to discover and expose traitors such as Donald. Once Yvonne had passed on her airmen, she would have no knowledge of what happened to them.

The airmen would not be going back to England as they had hoped. After interrogation, the three were detained and shared a small cell for a couple of weeks under terrible conditions. There were some tense moments when the Germans saw that both Shierlaw and Bush were carrying the same dog tag, and they were threatened with extreme punishment for covering their identities for nefarious purposes. But after a few days the threats stopped, presumably because the Germans were able to verify their identities. It was then on to an isolation cell in a Luftwaffe prison in Brussels for two days, after which the men were herded onto rail cars.

They were headed for prisoner-of-war camps. Lorne could not imagine what that would be like and tried not to dwell on an uncertain future, but to take each day as it came. He dearly hoped that his folks back home would be notified of his capture quickly and not believe he had perished in the crash.

CHAPTER TWELVE
Kingston
September 2005

Lorne opens the door of the little smoking cabinet beside his chair. Made by Gibbard Furniture in his hometown of Napanee, it had been a wedding gift to him and Ruth. Inside is his Wartime Log book, given to him by the War Prisoners' Aid of the YMCA in Geneva, Switzerland, when he had been interred. The inside cover says, "Issued to W/o Shetler L.M. 280/L7." He had been expected to record his life in the camp to assist his memory if he was lucky enough to return to Britain for a debriefing. As he leafs through the pages, the words blur but the memory is clear.

Excerpts from Lorne's log:

May 24–25, 1944

Shot down the night of the day on which we finished our seven days' leave, target Aachen, Germany. I thought it was a fighter but the WOp[45] says flak. The skipper, engineer and mid-upper gunner went down with the kite—poor devils. I landed in a small tree and then hit a stump, hurting my "rear end" and back. Walked until daylight and holed up. I found out later I was still in Holland near the Belgian border, not far from the coast.

---

45   Wireless Operator

May 25, 1944

Some good people gave me food and civilian clothes and I moved to some people connected with the underground and was in bed for four days unable to walk. Met up with some other fellows and moved around among farmers and houses in the neighbourhood. My rear end getting a little better. The doctors I saw gave me some stuff and said it was a matter of time to get better. It got hot after a few days and we left one morning 15 minutes before the German soldiers moved in to stay there. Three of us stayed there for three days and were there when the invasion started. Next day we rode bicycles for 20 miles, received Dutch passports and stayed at another place for several more days. Met Charlie Shierlaw of Rideau Park, Billings Bridge, Ottawa, and Walter Bush of 12 Erpingham Rd, Westbourne, Bournemouth, of one of our crews shot down a few miles from us, and moved with them to Belgium by bicycle. After crossing the border, we went by tram to Antwerp, where we holed up again about three days. Finally they told us we were being watched and moved us to another place.

June 15, 1944

It was a swell place and they gave us all we could eat and drink of the best to be had. A "bootlegger," a tall well-built blond man in a grey suit, a slight sallow man in a grey topcoat or raincoat, and a man in civvies, who later turned out to be a German prison guard, were our captors. They hauled us into a fine car and took us to the German military police. There we were searched and questioned about the underground and then taken to Antwerp prison. We were there for two weeks, not much to eat, very unsanitary conditions in a room 8' x 14', three of us. The swelling from my back settled in my left leg which hadn't been sore before and was very painful. I had treatment for the bug bites and crabs and massage and heat on my lame leg. They called us American gangsters and held us as spies in our civvies and with our forged Belgian passports. After two weeks they moved 21 of us to Brussels to a Luftwaffe prison where they kept us in solitary for a day or two. They gave us bogus Red Cross forms to fill out and told us all about ourselves.

July 1, 1944

They moved a whole carriage full of us to Frankfurt. It was very slow on account of the blasted railway yards. We left in the afternoon, got into Dusseldorf early the next a.m. and Frankfurt that p.m. At Dulag Luft we were stripped of our civvies and sent on to the transient camp at Wetzlar without any more interrogation. Here they gave us American clothes and some decent food from Red Cross parcels.

CHAPTER THIRTEEN
Napanee
Summer 1944

Life on the farm followed its usual patterns in the year after Lorne went overseas, as there was always much work to be done. Though Ethel allowed herself some moments of worry in the quiet of early morning, for the most part life went on as before. She wrote to him often, sending parcels without knowing whether they would arrive; she wanted him to have reminders of home. She treasured the letters she received from him. They would come sporadically, sometimes none for weeks and then two or three together.

While Stuart accepted Lorne's choice to go overseas and tried not to dwell on it, Ethel missed him and worried as only a mother could. Her sweet, handsome son. He had always been the thoughtful one and though he loved his five brothers, he had a special spot in his heart for sisters Helen and Hazel, and they for him. Helen had even named her first-born, Lorna, after him.

They heard the news of the June 6 D-Day invasion, heralded as the beginning of the end of the war. But not for their son. Although they didn't know it then, in many ways the worst had just begun for him.

On June 28, 1944, a telegram arrived to notify Ethel and Stuart that their son Lorne had been reported missing after a bombing mission to Aachen in late May. Time stood still at the news and Ethel felt as though she could hardly breathe. But the family would not let themselves believe the worst, and each day they prayed for news that he had been located and was on his way home. The town of Napanee prayed right along with them. Then, about two weeks later in mid-July, Ethel received a letter from the brother of one of Lorne's crew.

***

Letter from Bob "Jughead" Christie's brother to Ethel Shetler:

High Park Ave.
Toronto, ON

July 7, 1944

Mrs. Shetler,
My brother Bob was a member of the same crew as your son and we are anxious to hear if you have had any news of him since they were listed as missing. One of the other members, F/O Ronald Rudd, the navigator, has been reported prisoner of war in Germany. His home address is 1072 Third Ave. W., Owen Sound, Ont. The only news we have had of Bob is most disheartening but we are still hoping to hear he is safe. Especially now that we know one of the crew has turned up.

I knew your son as I was overseas as a pilot myself and returned the end of January. I visited the boys in my brother's crew often before leaving England.

I sincerely hope that you have had good news of your son and hope that all the crew turns up safely soon.

I am sending you a copy of the telegram we received yesterday.
We will be anxiously waiting to hear from you.

A friend of your son's,
Bruce Christie

***

A Good Man

Telegram:

> *We regret to advise, the International Red Cross quoting German information states your son Sgt. Robert F. Christie lost his life May 25, but does not give additional particulars. Pending further confirmation your son is to be considered missing, believed killed.*

***

Ethel looked at the date of the letter and fear gripped her heart. May 25. Lorne and his crew had been missing a whole month before the notification came that Sgt. Christie was officially missing and presumed dead. Was a similar telegram on its way to them at that very moment? She knew from Lorne's letters that Bob Christie had been the mid-upper gunner in his crew. Why was he presumed dead? How did they know? Where were the rest of the crew? Please God, she prayed, let the rest be safe.

She had kept every letter that Lorne sent home, pressed in the pages of a book. It helped now to take them out and read them and imagine that he was just now writing another to explain away her greatest fear.

Another week went by, and she told herself that no news was good news, as a telegram like the Christie family received had not yet arrived. And then, on July 27, the news they had prayed for:

Western Union to Canadian National Telegram, July 27, 1944
Ottawa, Ont.

Stuart Shetler
Napanee, Ont.

Pleased to advise International Red Cross quoting German information states your Son Warrant Officer second class Lorne Melvin Shetlor (sic) is a prisoner of War stop letter follows

RCAF Casualties Office

> R.   S.   8.25 A.M. 28th   30 Paid G.B. 2 ex
>
> Ottawa Ont.   July 27th/1944
>   Stuart Shetlor
>   Report Delivery R R # 7
>   Napanee Ont.
>
>   M 9209 Pleased to advise International Red Cross quoting German information states your Son Warrant Officer second class Lorne Melvin Shetlor is a prisoner of War stop letter follows.
>
>   R.C.A.F. Casualties Officer.

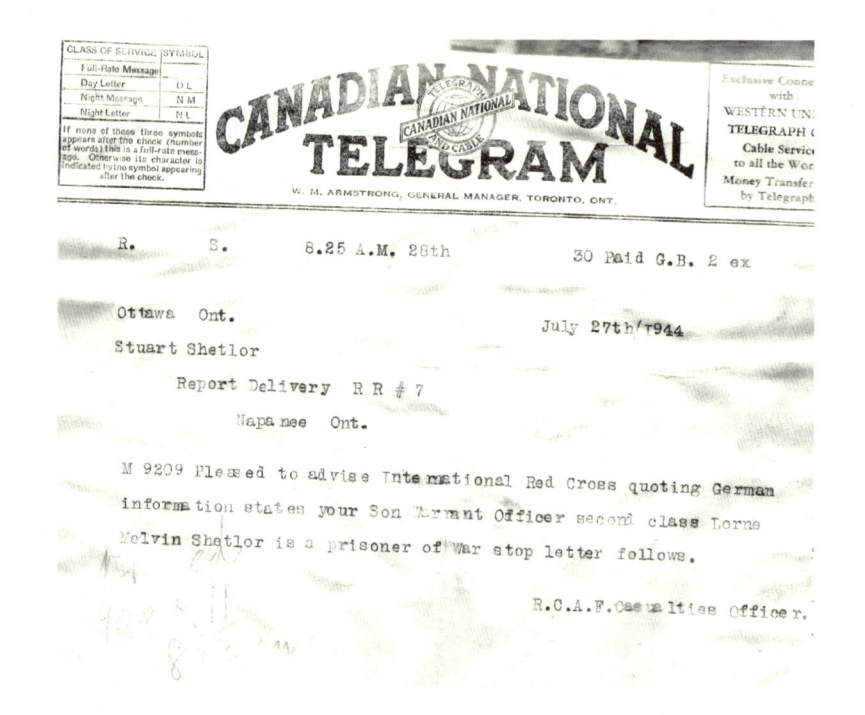

A photograph of the telegram sent to the Shetlers.

***

In September, another telegram arrived from the Red Cross, dated June 14, 1944, having taken a circuitous route from the POW camp, through the censors, and then to the Canadian Foreign Affairs Office where it was date stamped September 6, 1944, by an official examiner. Had this only arrived sooner, weeks of worry could have been avoided. But she didn't dwell on that now. She just read and reread the five comforting words. Lorne was alive and that was all she needed to know:

COMITE INTERNATIONAL DE LA CROIX-ROUGE
GENÈVE (Suisse)

Message (not over 25 words, family news of strictly personal character)

Dear folks. Am well and good health. Love Lorne

Date 14.6.44   Examined by D.B/80 September 6, 1944

A Good Man

COMITÉ INTERNATIONAL DE LA CROIX-ROUGE
GENÈVE (Suisse)

61

1 CM 206551

DEMANDEUR — ANFRAGESTELLER — ENQUIRER

Nom — Name: LORN.
Prénom — Vorname — Christian name: care of
Rue — Strasse — Street: Mme Anny Peter
Localité — Ortschaft — Locality: Alpine Institut
Département — Provinz — County: FETAN
Pays — Land — Country: Suisse   Grisons

Message à transmettre — Mitteilung — Message
(25 mots au maximum, nouvelles de caractère strictement personnel et familial) — (nicht über 25 Worte, nur persönliche Familiennachrichten) — (not over 25 words, family news of strictly personal character).

Dear folks. Am well and good health. Love Lorne

Date — Datum: 14.6.44   6 SEPT. 1944

DESTINATAIRE — EMPFÄNGER — ADDRESSEE

Nom — Name: Mrs. Shetler
Prénom — Vorname — Christian name: Stuart.
Rue — Strasse — Street:
Localité — Ortschaft — Locality: NAPANEE
Province — Provinz — County: Ontario
Pays — Land — Country: Canada

RÉPONSE AU VERSO   ANTWORT UMSEITIG   REPLY OVERLEAF
Prière d'écrire très lisiblement   Bitte sehr deutlich schreiben   Please write very clearly

A photograph of Lorne's message home, sent through the Red Cross.

Jeanie Quirt Brown

Lorne's POW photograph.

CHAPTER FOURTEEN
Germany
Summer 1944

Lorne's Log:

<u>July 6–10, 1944</u>

They loaded 40 RAF and colonials[46] in a small car and shipped us by freight to Bankeau, L.7.[47] It was very hot and cramped and we took turns sleeping in the aisle and under the seats at night. Our three-day rations ran out and they got us some soup from the German Red Cross.

<u>July 10, 1944</u>

Arrived at L.7 and were photographed again and given huts, six in each. Still sleep on the floor but plenty to eat thanks to the Red Cross.

Some kind of rash all over my body, was painted up like a zebra all summer. Finally cured by zinc ointment and calcium pills. Stiffness left my legs after a month or so but played softball just the same in the meantime.

***

---

46 RAF airmen from Commonwealth countries, now considered a derogatory term.

47 Stalag Luft VII was a prisoner-of-war camp for commissioned and non-commissioned flying officers, located in Bankau, Silesia, Germany (now Poland). There were approximately 1,600 prisoners. Stalag was short for "Stammlager," a German term used for prisoner-of-war camps.

July 12, 1944

Dear Folks:
Here I am getting settled down at last on a permanent POW camp. My address is under "absender"[48] *on outside. Everyone leads a very lazy life here with plenty of fresh air and sunshine and we do not work. Each man gets one Red Cross parcel per week, so along with what the Germans provide we get plenty to eat and drink. There are 50 to 100 American or English cigarettes in each parcel. You can consult the Red Cross about letter writing. I do not think it is worthwhile to try to send me parcels but wish you would help out the Red Cross with money. How are you all coming? OK I hope, like I have been since being taken the middle of June. Will drop you another line later on in the month.*

Love to all,
Lorne

***

August 3, 1944

Dear Folks,
Just a line to let you know I'm still alive and kicking. Things go along much the same here from day to day so there's really no news to speak of. We live a lot of the time in the open air and the weather is much as it is at home. Plenty of rain lately. I'm getting tanned like an Indian and have been playing a lot of softball for exercise. We are not allowed to work so all we have to do is wash our own dishes, peel spuds, etc. Have enough food but are short on all toilet articles and not too many clothes. We are allowed two letters per month so will write again later on. Hope you've heard I'm POW so don't worry about me. Hope you are all well and that you are not working too hard. Hope to have a line from you soon,

Love,
Lorne

---

48 "Sender" in German, indicating the return address.

A Good Man

***

September 15, 1944

Dear Folks:
Just a line to say that I'm still alive and kicking. Weather is fine but nights are beginning to get chilly. All okay here and hope it's the same with you. Hope you're all in good health.

Love,
Lorne

***

Lorne's Log:

October 13, 1944

Moved to new camp on Friday 13th with 14 men going in a room about 18' x 30'. Moved two extra men in about Armistice, making three survivors of First Armoured Division in our room (Arnhem[49] lot) and Harry Davis.

***

October 28, 1944

Dear Folks,
Things are pretty quiet here right now so I thought I'd drop a line before afternoon parade. There's a bridge tournament going on in the camp, so we played off another match today. They're fixing up a sports field here at our new camp, but since softball season is finished, we play a lot of bridge and cards and read books. Our appetites are really good so we sort of wait from one meal to the next, but we get enough to eat, with an issue of Red Cross parcels either every one or two weeks. Needless to say, our bit of chocolate and cigs go fast. Some of the boys have had letters and I'm hoping for some

---

49 The battle of Arnhem (September 17–25, 1944) was a failed attempt to establish a bridgehead across the lower Rhine River at the Dutch town of Arnhem.

in the near future. Hope you're all well; needless to say, I'm in first class shape and waiting patiently.

Love,
Lorne

***

Royal Canadian Air Force
Ottawa, Canada

November 11, 1944

Mr. Stuart Shetler
Napanee, Ontario

Dear Mr. Shetler:
It is a pleasure to advise you that your son, Lorne Melvin Shetler, who is a Prisoner of War in Germany, has been commissioned with the rank of Pilot Officer with effect from May 9, 1944. His Officer's number is J86643.

Notification of the promotion has been forwarded to the Department of External Affairs, Ottawa, for transmission to your son.

Yours sincerely,
W.M. Widmer
RCAF Casualty Officer
For Chief of the Air Staff

***

Lorne's Log:

November 29, 1944

Issue of heavy trousers. Started work on skating rink. Enough parcels to last until Christmas, half parcel per man per week. Boys out playing English Rugby in the mud.

***

A Good Man

December 7, 1944

Dear Folks:

Just received two letters and was really glad to hear from you and know you are okay. Your letter was dated September 10 and Hazel's was October 21. Six months seems a long while to wait for news. Glad to hear about the parcel but not too sure that they'll get through. Nice to hear about Edison Unger getting home. Too bad about Ferdie, Bob and Mac though, wish you could say the same for them. Glad to hear that you're taking at least a few day's holidays. It will do you and Daddy both a lot of good.

There is nothing new here except we're fixing up an open-air skating rink. The weather is still nice here though and I hope we're never able to use it. Hazel said you got one of my letters; hope you soon get more. Thanks for writing, it was a nice Christmas present. Hope you're still all well.

Love,
Lorne

***

Lorne's Log:

<u>December 27, 1944</u>

Yanks bomb almost every day at noon between spud and soup time. They have shot at fellows for venturing out during an air raid, but hit nobody.

This time Len Stevenson, a Canuck from Dawson Creek, Saskatchewan, was shot and died shortly after the "all clear" had gone at Kreuzburg but not at the camp—range 100 yards—"a very regrettable incident."

CHAPTER FIFTEEN
The Long March
January 2–February 8, 1945

Letter to Lorne's Mom, January 2, 1945:

I never expected to spend a New Year in one of these places but here I am still. There's nothing unusual in the way of food or anything except we've saved up and made a cake. Needless to say it didn't agree with most of the boys the next day, even though they were good at the time. We had special Christmas services but only Mass today.

Having nice winter weather and snow. Our rink is all ready now but we lack skates and hockey stuff; we hope to get our Christmas food parcels sometime too. I got my fifth letter the other day and am looking forward to more letters and those parcels. Some Canucks have had them from September and October but cigarettes seem awfully scarce. Well, I hope you all have a very Happy and Prosperous New Year and hope to see you before the next one.

Love to all,
Lorne

***

Lorne's Log:

January 7, 1945

War not over yet and I owe Dave Banning a bottle of Scotch when I get back. Counted four times on parade and twice in our room. The boys registered as Jews have been moved into a room in 88 Division. Search at 11:30 at night of Eighth Division and they went straight to a tunnel started. One discovered before from massage room in Admin Block right out to the wire. Searches are a common occurrence. Good winter weather. Not too cold.

January 17, 1945

Joe[50] getting close. Big Jerry[51] evacuation on the way. At 11:00 a.m. orders to be ready to move in an hour. All kinds of trucks and wagons on the road. Told in afternoon parade we'll probably move early in morning. Bags of Jerry rations brought in and whole camp sacked by POWs. Move didn't come off.

January 18, 1945

Lined up in marching columns. Finally went back in barracks and told to be ready at 3:30 the next morning.

***

Lorne could not have imagined what lay ahead. Until now, life in the camp had been pretty routine. Food was adequate, if not plentiful, and they received Red Cross parcels on a semi-regular basis. Left to their own resources with no requirement to work, the boys made their own fun. A skating rink and sports field allowed for some competitive activity despite the shortage of real equipment. They were inventive, and fresh air was preferable to the barracks. Lorne had always loved playing cards, and here he had learned the game of bridge and had lots of willing partners for a game or tournament. There was no shortage

---

50   The Russian army was sometimes referred to as Joe or Uncle Joe, for Joseph Stalin.

51   Slang for German.

of paperback novels to read. All of these activities helped to relieve the boredom of the day-to-day routines.

There were times the boys were amused by what they saw as the stupidity of their captors. The guys would use the term "The Master Race" with great sarcasm. One day the prisoners were kept on parade because someone had taken the cook's revolver, until it was finally discovered that one of his ferrets had taken it. Another day they were kept on parade because the same cook had misplaced his butcher knife. A few months prior, one of the guards almost shot himself while changing the clip of bullets in his gun at the changing of the guard. Great cries had gone up around the camp, "Get some in."

Their captors suspected there was a tunnel in the camp. One night they came around in the rain at 11:30 pm with a flashlight and checked the prisoners' photos. They looked at Lorne twice because he looked so much different without all the hair and whiskers he had sported when his POW picture had been taken. For some reason they were also very suspicious of the outhouse and had guards and dogs in the camp at night watching.

One of the boys was late to parade one day and upon arrival gave his name as Whitehall 1212. Overnight the guards realized that this was the number for Scotland Yard. They had fallen for the prank, and they raised the devil over it.

Despite the untrusting relationship between the German guards and their prisoners, they were willing to barter for food and items that were scarce at the time. Starvation was a deliberate policy in many of the camps, but more for the Russian POWs than the British, Canadians, or Americans. The much-anticipated Red Cross parcels provided them with palatable food as well as currency for trading. They typically contained tins of jam, chocolate bars, sugar, coffee, biscuits, powdered milk, some form of canned meat and cigarettes. In Lorne's camp, some of the prisoners traded chocolate and soap from the packages for a radio. They had to keep it out of sight, but it allowed them to keep up with what was taking place outside the strands of barbed wire. It also offered some hope that the Allies were making progress despite the demoralizing propaganda continually broadcast over the camp speakers, always claiming the Nazis were close to winning the war.

Lorne assumed this place would be his home until the war was over and thought, "It could be worse."

And it did become worse very soon. Between January and April 1945, with Allied forces advancing on the Eastern Front, there began what would later be called "The Long March" and other similar monikers. The Germans began to evacuate POW camps and forced the Allied prisoners to march westward across Poland, keeping ahead of the Soviet Army. Lorne was one of an estimated 80,000 prisoners who joined hundreds of thousands of German refugees travelling on foot in extreme weather conditions, reportedly one of the harshest winters in a century. They were woefully ill-prepared for the sub-zero Fahrenheit temperatures and swirling blizzards. Without adequate winter clothing and with rations dwindling, many men dropped out or died along the way.

Sleep was elusive as they rested in mostly unheated barns and outbuildings, and yet they were roused early each morning, in darkness, to march 20 to 40 kilometres each day. The food allocation was not nearly enough to sustain an adult, let alone these men who trudged so far day after day. The POWs were plagued by dysentery and lice but had to keep moving or risk being left behind or shot. As temperatures rose above zero, some prisoners began to discard heavy coats or blankets along the way because they were just too heavy for them to carry in their weakened state.

Lorne continued his daily entries in his war log, but the entries were brief and his writing harder to read as his hands were numb from cold. He began to record the day of the week along with the date, his one way to keep track of time as one day blended into the next.

They did not know at the time, but it would later become clear that while they were enduring these long marches and horrible freezing temperatures, nearby there were worse atrocities being committed. In a parallel world, untold numbers of Jews, as well as Gypsies, homosexuals and disabled persons, were also being marched or shipped in railway cars across Poland and Germany. They were also headed for camps, extermination camps, and the majority would not survive.

A Good Man

***

Lorne's Log:

January 19, 1945

Flashes in the sky. Roused out at 3:30 a.m. and left around 7 a.m. A 40-mile-per-hour wind blowing. Went thru Kreuzberg Constadt (sp?) and spent night in Winterbel and quartered in barns. No hot drink. Ration of bread 2/3 loaf. Twenty-four kilometres.

January 20, 1945

Started out at 4 a.m. Got to a factory around noon and stayed for the afternoon and had hot drinks. Started marching at 8 p.m. and marched all night. Cold, around zero, and foggy. Around 100 guys dropped out from exposure, etc. Crossed our objective, the Oder River, and arrived at village at dawn.

January 21, 1945

No quarters here so went on to a barn seven kilometres further. Covering 35 kilometres altogether. Spent day there and had good sleep in the cow barn and hot drinks.

January 22, 1945

Roused at 4:00 a.m. and left later on. Two hundred tried to stay but were threatened and shots fired. Nobody hurt but all came along. Twenty deserted by now and 15 left for hospital. Panic on the road—army, civilians, etc. Heard Ruskies took Strasbourg[52] and leveled Bankau at noon on the 19th. Everybody hungry—issued a bag of hardtack.[53] Arrived at another barn around noon and spent night in a cowshed. Pretty cold. Issued with half a biscuit and marg,[54] and half cup warm stew.

---

52 A city on the eastern border of France with Germany.

53 A simple biscuit or cracker made from flour, water, and sometimes salt, often used in military campaigns because it is inexpensive and long-lasting.

54 Margarine

January 23, 1945

Marched at 7 a.m. with a crust of bread left and a handful of beans from the floor, uncooked.

Road littered with refugees and dead horses were lying along the way. Feel kind of sorry for all these people. Snowing some and all are cold and stumbling along from lack of food. Went about 25 kilometres and reached another barn and had warm stew, half cup each. Good warm shed to sleep in.

January 24, 1945

Made a brew in morning on little fire and had beans and wheat. Cookhouse gave us a barley stew, half cup each, and we got frozen spuds, seven roasted in fire. Issued one-quarter loaf of fresh bread.

January 25, 1945
(Passed Strehlen)

Roused out at 2:00 in morning. Marched until 2:00 pm to another farm, at Heidersdorf, 32 kilometres. Met boys from Lamsdorf,[55] camp bombed and strafed on road, ten killed and many wounded. Still hear guns—six cigars from Jerry and two ounces tea for bread.

January 26, 1945

Laid over a day and scrounged spuds, beans, and ate soup powder found day before. Seventy-six thousand POWs on the road.

Saturday, January 27, 1945

Two Frenchies say Breslau taken. Moved out around noon. Covered 18 kilometres. Managed to bum a few cigs. Stopped at a barn in horse stable. Hard walking. Sagan, five days [away].

---

55 Stalag VIII-B Lamsdorf, later renumbered Stalag-344, was a POW camp located near the village of Lamsdorf in Silesia.

Sunday, January 28, 1945

[Up at] 2:00 a.m. Made 22 kilometres by noon to another barn. Snow and cold. Passed thru Schweidnitz. No fires allowed and no rations. Slept in horse stable, uncomfortable and cold.

Monday, January 29, 1945

Cold whole wheat for breakfast. Snow hung around all day and marched at 5:00 p.m. Blowing a small blizzard. Traffic hung up and corpse along road. Promised porridge and train at end of today's march, but porridge spilt and no train. Cold barn at 3:00–4:00 a.m. near Jever.

Tuesday, January 30, 1945

Had a fire most of day cooking spuds, what we could scrounge. Very cold again at night.

Wednesday, January 31, 1945

Rose 7:15 a.m. and made brew. Roll call at noon. Told Sagan had been evacuated and we will march 18 kilometres the next day to Goldberg and told we might get a train. Cold and miserable. Hear booms all night and morning and flashes in the sky.

Thursday, February 1, 1945

Very sloppy underfoot and mild. Rose at 6:30 and reached a barn a few kilometres from Goldberg at noon. Got two-fifths of a loaf of bread.

Friday, February 2, 1945

Still mild. Made brew. Received one potato per man. Waiting for transport from Goldberg.

Saturday, February 3, 1945

Still quite mild out. Still no transport. Had a shave and a cleanup. Ruskies supposed to be 60 kilometres from Berlin.

Sunday, February 4, 1945

Cooler—windy. Rumour of 15–20 wagons.[56] One-sixth loaf of bread and brew. Church services. Cheers at news of train.

Monday, February 5, 1945

Roused out at 4 a.m., mild and rainy. In train at Goldberg seven kilometres away by 9:30. Moved to Liegnitz and stayed night in cars at Sagan. Very cramped. Fifty-four in car.

Tuesday, February 6, 1945

Moved on a little farther. No water—allowed out for five minutes in morning. About two to three hours' run.

Wednesday, February 7, 1945

Getting hungry, thirsty, very crowded. Half cup of brew in p.m.

Thursday, February 8, 1945

Another hell of a night in car. Still no food or water. Taken out around noon to Stammlager III-A[57]. Given bath and food and bed on floor. Glory Be! Barbed wire again at Luckenwalde.

---

56 Rail cars

57 Also known as Stalag III-A, a POW camp located at Luckenwalde, Brandenburg, 52 kilometres south of Berlin

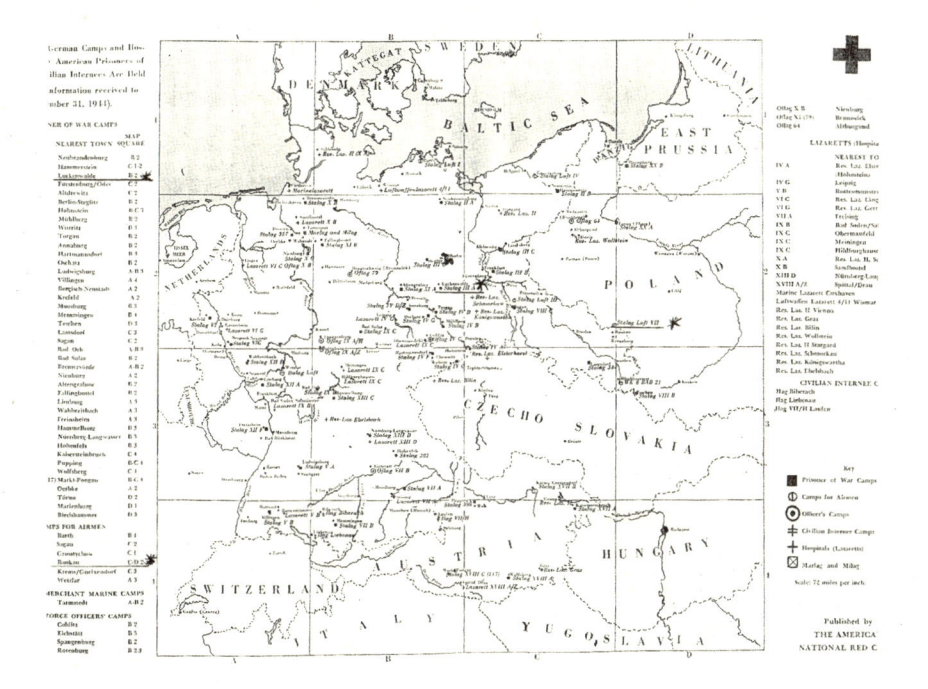

POW camp locations mapped by the American Red Cross. Lorne began the long march at Stalag Luft VII near Bankau (C–D2) and ended at Stalag III-A near Luckenwalde (B2).

***

From Lorne's diary: "Out on the road, January 1945"

The snow wasn't very deep and it was about 20 degrees Fahrenheit in daytime. We stayed in barns at night and they gave us hot gruel. After three weeks they loaded us in cattle cars and we ended up a way out of Berlin. The sign on the cattle car read "8 horses or 40 men," or in our case 200 POWs. I found out later that the ones who had to drop out on our walk were looked after. Some deserted for the Russian lines and I never heard how they made out.

There were 30,000 men in different compounds in that camp. Ron Rudd was in an officers' compound across the way; he had walked in from the north. At least the building had a wooden floor and there was room to lie down. I had two blankets and my bridge playing partner, "Keller," Joel from Vancouver, had one. He had dropped one on the march, too heavy to carry. We had to sleep in our clothes for warmth and he shared my blankets.

CHAPTER SIXTEEN
Luckenwalde, Germany Winter 1945

Lorne's Log:

Friday, February 9, 1945

Two-fifths of loaf and drippings. Feeling better. Had a shave, Irish Guards helping out a little.

Saturday, February 10, 1945

Reveille 6:00, roll call 7:15. Had a haircut.

Sunday, February 11, 1945

Photo check—dirty and rainy out, did a little washing.

Monday, February 12, 1945

Sent my boots in[58] through George Howe. Photo check again.

Tuesday, February 13, 1945

Little more chilly.

Coffee from George!

---

58 Lorne noted in a newspaper interview in 2002 that he had worn out his boots by the end of the Long March, and they did not have any soles left. It is unclear where he sent them to be repaired or who George Howe was.

Wednesday, February 14, 1945

Boots repaired with wooden soles.

Thursday, February 15, 1945

[Date recorded, but no written entry.]

Friday, February 16, 1945

The Red Cross rep here today. Said no chance of being moved to a neutral country and conditions would probably be worse. No parcels. Bread ration cut to one-seventh of loaf.

Saturday, February 17, 1945

224 men on parade—190 in barracks. A Group Captain coming in this afternoon to see us. Made a pancake from potato flour, water and sugar.

Sunday, February 18, 1945

Little colder—no circulation in hands and feet. Lying in sack.

Monday, February 19, 1945

Rumour of parcels.

Tuesday, February 20, 1945

No parcels. Did a little walking, issue of Jerry soap, washed my underwear.

Wednesday, February 21, 1945

Wrote a letter card for a change. Rainy and chilly out.

Thursday, February 22, 1945

Washed a shirt and shaved. [There was a] cut in spud and soup ration. Expect a pack of smokes from Lost Parcel Dept.

Friday, February 23, 1945

Issue of 22 cigs and bit of tobacco. And a bit of Red Cross stuff.

Saturday, February 24, 1945

Took off my long underwear and washed it. Diarrhea a little better (I hope).

Monday, February 26, 1945

Miserable and rainy. Issue of salt. Traded my marg ration (1/20 lb) for two cigs.

Tuesday, February 27, 1945

Lay in sack all day. Air raid at night as usual. Berlin, eight nights in a row and some days, by Yanks.

Wednesday, February 28, 1945

Red Cross Parcel stores raided by three RAF last night in air raid. One wounded twice and another once. Soup high with salted pig again but eatable. Good news. Weather is mild.

Thursday, March 1, 1945

Birthday.[59]

Army took over Luft 7 today. After promising us a short parade, it took an hour and 15 minutes. Lay in sack. Promised one-quarter parcel each tomorrow or day after. Turkey[60] enters war today. Finished up my cigarette supply.

Friday, March 2, 1945

Very windy and cold out. Lay in sack with gloves on hands. Numb. Eighteen hundred parcels came in to French and they refused us any so Jerries confiscated some for our use.

---

59 Lorne's 28th.

60 Turkey had severed its diplomatic and commercial relations with Germany, and on February 23, 1945, declared war on Germany. Lorne would not have heard the news for a few days.

Saturday, March 3, 1945

Two roll calls in morning with blanket check. Expect issue of one-quarter parcel at 1:30 p.m. Received it at 6:30 p.m. At once ate three biscuits, cheese, pâté, salmon and meat and veg. Sold milk and jam. Saving chocolate, prunes, and coffee to sell.

Sunday, March 4, 1945

Snowing heavily. Working hard on rest of parcel and cigs. Bought tobacco pouch from Shorty Lapointe[61] for five cigs.

Monday, March 5, 1945

Very chilly in barracks. Cooked up my prunes and ate them—very good.

Tuesday, March 6, 1945

Some dirty lowdown thievin' _____ last night swiped my singlet out of my bag containing my knife, spoon, bread, marg, salt, etc., and my last pack of Camels. So when bread, sugar, etc., came up I woofed them. All my good containers gone.

Wednesday, March 7, 1945

A really beautiful day out. Had a shave and went for a walk. No lights last night. Berlin raided for 15th time in succession.

---

61 Per Michael Moores LeBlanc, F/Sgt Harold D. "Shorty" Lapointe of 429 Squadron was the only survivor of his aircraft, which was shot down just after leaving its target. As Shorty descended from his position of mid-upper gunner to bail out of the aircraft, he stepped in a hole in the fuselage floor caused by flak damage. His leg became stuck and his crew delayed their own evacuations to rescue him. The aircraft exploded and Shorty landed in a haystack, the only one to survive. He burrowed his way into the haystack with a badly broken leg and hid for two days before being discovered and captured. He could never forgive himself for the other men's deaths. The war never ended for him.

A Good Man

Thursday, March 8, 1945

Berlin got it again. Eighty thousand Red Cross parcels in. Received an issue of one each. Really got full for the first time since we left Bankau. Issue of 16 cigs. Buckshee.[62]

Friday, March 9, 1945

Berlin again—good news—more parcels reported, 16–18 cars. Made a makeshift blower from Klim tins,[63] and had big fry-up of spam and spuds and four brews of coffee.

Saturday, March 10, 1945

Berlin raided again. Sixteen more carloads of parcels at station—an issue for two more weeks, making five altogether.

Sunday, March 11, 1945

Very mild—prunes, Klim and sugar for breakfast again—wizard.[64]

Berlin again last night.

Monday, March 12, 1945

As usual—ready for another parcel issue. Berlin again.

Tuesday, March 13, 1945

Berlin again. Received parcel issue. Sardines, cereal and cocoa for a change. Heated two dixies of water at George's, washed myself and shirt.

Wednesday, March 14, 1945

Berlin again. Shaved. Took off my long underwear. Just like spring.

---

62   A British term for windfall.

63   Klim was a powdered milk from the Red Cross. Its metal cans were put to various uses in the camps, including as makeshift cookstoves.

64   A British slang term used by the airmen meaning excellent.

Thursday, March 15, 1945

Two hundred Irish working commandos moved out, including George Howe, Chalkey White, John and Hurley. More Yanks going too. Berlin raided.

Friday, March 16, 1945

Berlin raided. Had a very short brush-cut. Nice spring day. Crown and anchor games, etc., for cigs all about.

Saturday, March 17, 1945

Berlin again. Shaved. Spud ration now every other day. Bread cut to six men to a small loaf. St. Patrick's Day. Soccer games, etc., with Irish. X-ray of our chests for tuberculosis.

Sunday, March 18, 1945

Carrier for soup, etc. New blower works bang on. Berlin again but blackout at 8:45 last night, 45 minutes later than normal.

Monday, March 19, 1945

Bread seven men to loaf. No marg, spuds, etc. Two cups of soup at 5:00. Berlin raided for the 27th successive night. Three loads of Canadian parcels came in.

Tuesday, March 20, 1945

Berlin again. Parcel issue day. Shaved. Not quite as nice out.

Wednesday, March 21, 1945

Berlin again.

Thursday, March 22, 1945

Berlin again. Nice day. All kinds of games of chance going around. Had a bath and washed my clothes.

Friday, March 23, 1945

Berlin raided. Nice weather. Rations cut to eight men to a loaf and cut in marg and sugar.

Saturday, March 24, 1945

Spud ration cut in half. Eight men to a loaf again. Cleaned out wood and straw. In future sleep on floor.

Sunday, March 25, 1945

Berlin raided for 33rd successive night. More air raids early this a.m. Seven to a loaf, bought Jerry sausage for 150 fags—I got half split wood from wood party. Ordered a copy of *The Road Back*.[65] Went to a soccer game. France won 1–0.

Monday, March 26, 1945

Berlin raided. Two soups. No spuds.

Tuesday, March 27, 1945

Berlin for 35th successive night. Parcel issue today. Enough on hand for two more issues and then some over.

Wednesday, March 28, 1945

Meeting of Canadian Club and jam session in the morning.

Friday, March 30, 1945

Berlin raided. Did a washing and had a bath. Good Friday.

Saturday, March 31, 1945

Cold and slightly miserable.

Sunday, April 1, 1945

Easter Sunday. Went to Anglo-Catholic Communion. Big football game in the afternoon.

Monday, April 2

Changed over to daylight time. Windy with a lot of dust and rain squalls like at Bankau last summer.

---

65 A novel by German writer Erich Maria Remarque about the experiences of young men returning from the trenches of the First World War. It is a sequel of sorts to his book *All Quiet on the Western Front*.

Tuesday, April 3, 1945

Parcel issue postponed on account of Easter Monday holiday. "Hard knockin'." Rainy and miserable.

Wednesday, April 4, 1945

Berlin raided, 100 British and French POWs killed as Yanks raided Brandenburg. Parcel issue and gash[66] issue of 20 cigs from Lost Parcels.

Thursday, April 5, 1945

Made pudding of bread, K2[67] biscuits, sugar, marg, Klim, cocoa—very good. Carrier for soup. Berlin raided.

Friday, April 6, 1945

Berlin raided, rainy and miserable. Three loads of parcels but two sent on to III-B to guys who had been on road for 54 days. Enough on hand for half or two issues. Had a two-hour identity check in the afternoon. They took us all out in another field, called our numbers and checked our photos and tags as we passed back into the compound.

Saturday, April 7, 1945

Buckshee issue of 65 cigs (Camels). Managed to buy one pack of Briar and Old Virginia pipe tobacco for 155 cigs.

Sunday, April 8, 1945

Played softball with Yanks. Beat them 6–1. Yank Thunderbolts[68] over.

Monday, April 9, 1945

Quite miserable out again. Usual air raid at night. Three loads of parcels in, enough for two complete issues. Received an issue of matches and cigarette papers. Eight men to a loaf and stinking yellow cheese, double

---

66   "Gash" has been used in other POW journals to describe leftover food.

67   A graham biscuit included in K-rations.

68   The P-47, known as a Thunderbolt, was a single-engine fighter and fighter-bomber aircraft used by the Allies.

skillet ration of barley and no spuds. Sixty-five promotions and commissions put up on the board; my new number is J86643.

Tuesday, April 10, 1945

Bathed and washed some clothes. Had lottery for Canadian clothes and food but got nothing but two squares chocolate and gum. Parcel issue okay. Told to be ready to move to Oflag[69] at 2000 hours but didn't move.

---

69 From the German "Offizierslager": a prisoner of war camp for officers.

CHAPTER SEVENTEEN
Luckenwalde
Spring 1945

Wednesday, April 11, 1945

Standing by at 1000 hours to move from camp but didn't go. Traded Spam for cheese and pâté. Broke crystal and hour hand off my watch last night and lost without it. Made raisin and prune jam—not bad. Warned to be ready to move to the south with 300 RAF NCOs by rail at 8:00 a.m.

Thursday, April 12, 1945

Started counting the boys out around 10:30. We were all packed but when it wasn't announced in our barracks six officers didn't show up. McGinty threatened trouble and to call out the guard. We finally went but missed the search so kept our water bottles, blankets, un-punctured tins, etc. Put in [rail] cars, 40 to each, and given half a parcel (no. 10) each and gash issue of 40 cigs (Camels). Had a good sleep all lying stretched on our sides after a brew cup.

Friday, April 13, 1945

Two boys, RAF and RCAF, attempted to get thru wire. One killed and the other seriously wounded, died later on. Spent day cooking, etc. Jerry brought us hot water, soup and spuds, bread and sausage. Shunted to another siding in the morning, still waiting for an engine. Rumour confirmed at night of a move back to camp since our way to south was cut off. Thunderbolts and Lightnings[70] flew over below cloud level and bombed next station. All Froggies,[71] Poles and Eyteys[72] in town trading bread, saccharin, spuds, eggs, etc., for cigs, soap, etc. Had another good sleep in [rail] car. F.D. Roosevelt kicked the bucket.

Saturday, April 14, 1945

Prepared and moved back to camp about 2:30 p.m. Brewed in meantime. Talked to Ron Rudd and Tug Thomson and Lee Caunt of Charlie's and Wally's crew. Dave Benning got two 2-kilo loaves for 80 cigs and a half can of coffee, and I got 100 saccs[73] for a bar of soap. Heavy luggage hauled back by transport. Rations up at Barrack 35 and bed in 9N. An awful muddle but by bedtime had double barley skillet, bread and marg. Parcel issue cut to half parcel per week and three more cars at station.

Never figured I'd be glad to get behind the barbed wire of the same camp twice. Hope they have us here this time until we're finally relieved.

Sunday, April 15, 1945

Close air raid last night (looked about 30 miles but close enough for me).

Really wizard display, bright night, flak, search lights, photo flashes, flares and our windows shook. About an hour on parade with 35, two more name checks before breakfast. Gash issue of food from Canadian parcels up (bit of coffee and chocolate).

At funeral of two men who tried to escape, RAF dressed in clean uniforms, wreaths made by Froggies. The fat boy from our barracks even went with a nice bunch of Easter lilies. Buried in local "Kriegie"[74] cemetery.

---

70 The Lockheed P-38, also known as a Lightning, was an American fighter and fighter-bomber aircraft.

71 A slang word for French.

72 A slang word for Italians.

73 Saccharin, a sugar substitute.

74 A term for Allied prisoners of war in German camps.

Monday, April 16, 1945

Drew half parcel with Dave Balchum to last for two weeks. Going to be hard knockin' for my other half is almost kaput. Received one-eighth loaf fresh bread, marg, and beet. Ran out of bread and marg but they got some more from Luckenwalde. Got back on ration strength of 9N again. Continual air alarm.

Wednesday, April 18, 1945

Air fresher after a thunderstorm last night which I never even heard. Played a game of catch with Killer. Got gash issue of 25 sweet caps and received 500 [cigarettes] from Canada Breweries, my first parcel. 150 men from Lamsdorf arrived in camp. They were left from 400 who left in January [on the Long March] and figured they covered 1,000 miles on foot. The MO[75] put them on diet parcels right away considering their condition.

Thursday, April 19, 1945

Took up a collection of cigs for boys from Lamsdorf. Enough parcels on hand for one between five men (Canadian). Very windy, stayed inside.

Friday, April 20, 1945

Big air operations close at hand. Bombing and smoke clouds. Continual alert. Went to a football game between Camp and French. Bought Half and Half tobacco for 60 cigs and wood for six. All kinds of rumours.

Saturday, April 21, 1945

Wilder rumours yet of Ruskies and Yanks being close. Boom of artillery. No roll call and people rushing all over. Jerries evacuating all night. Our officers in control of cookhouse and Jerry officers gone. Stored some water in case of shortage. Rainy day—knocked out Ruskie tank crew brought into camp by Jerry guards. All kinds of looting going on for a while. Ruskies raided a potato dump and are really "in rackets."[76]

---

75   Medical Officer

76   In a good position to barter or sell.

A wing commander took over parade and says we're practically surrounded, fighting in Juterburg and Luckenwalde. Paddy and I got two boxes of spuds from Ruskies for 70 cigs and sardines. Gash issue of 40 cigs. SS made everyone come in and announced there might be a search for guns looted from armoury and that 100 men would be shot for each gun found. Our five Jerry captives had to be released from cooler. Fighters did some strafing early after dark.

CHAPTER EIGHTEEN
Luckenwalde
Late April 1945

Sunday, April 22, 1945

Luckenwalde taken without fighting during the night. Liberation Day! When Jerry picked us up they said, "For you the war is over." But I guess they were slightly wrong.

Told to stay in on account of mortar fire into compound from east. Joe's men[77] came in with a flak gun and big celebration down below. Joe's fighters overhead, dive-bombing the Jerries. At about 1000 hours, two medium tanks and truck after truck with men and guns rolled in. What a reception they got! Cigarettes flying, cheering. Mostly young fellows and looked good and healthy. They demonstrated by clearing a barbed-wire fence away with a tank. They finally left and a Soviet Union commandant came up in the afternoon and promised us food, etc., in a few days. Cabbage soup and nothing else today but one-quarter of a No. 10.[78] The water and lights are off but water from our well can be used with boiling. At parade, the wing commander said the Norwegian General Otto Ruger had gone away for a while but they

---

77   Russian soldiers

78   10-in-1 rations offered one day of meals—breakfast, midday snack and evening supper—for 10 soldiers.

promised to leave us here until the Yanks come. Ruskie picked off by a sniper. Boys slit trenches watching Jerry fighter strafing and S.U.[79] flak.

Monday, April 23, 1945

Fighting not so close this morning but windows shook most of the night. Flak from nearby woods going at a Jerry fighter before breakfast. Early morning brew—no late info on news. Wings had parade—told us Ruskies had taken a place 15 miles west of us and this area under iron control. General Ruger gone to see Konev.[80] Allotted a town for food—plenty of meat but not much bread or spuds. Still confined to camp boundaries—three Froggies killed by S.4 patrol for not obeying an order. One Yank stabbed and another shot by Itaes.[81]

Tuesday, April 24, 1945

Trucks brought in enough meat for four days and bread for two. Jerry fighter strafing last night. News is good and lights are now on. Oflag,[82] Yanks', and NCOs' compounds made into one. Issue of one-quarter Canadian parcel coming up. Had conflab with Ronnie [Ron Rudd]. One-eighth loaf coming up, soup, meat, and butter.

Wednesday, April 25, 1945—San Francisco Conference [83]

Joe sent up one parcel each for Yanks and us, but following our rules we split with the other nationalities so we only get one-quarter parcel. Really liked the Canadian butter, Neilson's chocolate, jam and biscuits and lit into them.

When Jerry pulled out, we found eight Ruskies buried in refuse in their compound, dead from starvation. They had a big funeral this

---

79 Soviet Union

80 General Ivan Konev, Marshal of the Soviet Union.

81 Slang for Italians.

82 A German prison camp for captured enemy officers.

83 On this date the United Nations Conference on International Organization, commonly known as the San Francisco Conference, began, bringing together delegates from 50 Allied nations and resulting in the creation and signing of the United Nations Charter.

afternoon. Went across the way and watched Yanks fishing guns and shells out of the pond. Gash issue of 40 cigs up and a lot more on the way. Soviet Union Commandant sending up 40 radios and plenty of food promised.

Thursday, April 26, 1945

Water and light now on, waiting for news of a link-up but nothing happened. Two Yanks and woman newspaper reporter on way to Berlin promised to stop in.

Friday, April 27, 1945

Eleven thousand Jerries broke out of Berlin and headed southeast. They were stopped near here and heavy fighting took place before they were subdued or scattered in groups. They were all prepared to move us in the middle of the night but it didn't come off.

Went into Luckenwalde with Jack Friday and an Aussie. Going there is forbidden but the town is full of Kreigies. White flags all over and people wearing red or white arm bands. Steady stream of Russian-driven USA trucks and artillery going through towards Berlin, 58 kilometres away. Got knapsacks, canteen, 1,000 grams of Jerry coffee, corn flour, rhubarb, and onions and apples free for the looting. Paddy went another way and got 20 pounds of sugar.

Saturday, April 28, 1945

Raining out but Paddy and I went into Frankenfeld and scrounged fresh milk, rhubarb, briquettes of coal and more sugar. The boys are eating everything here: eggs, chicken, etc. Were chased out twice by a Ruskie with a rifle and could hear gunfire quite close. Parties of armed Jerries all around this sector.

Men are now allowed to go walking with an officer in sight of camp. Foraging parties go out every day and get food. They take half a farmer's supply of spuds, etc., and if he is found lying, they take the whole works. Rations of meat and pea soup, one-fifth loaf, 25 grams spud flour, 50 grams sugar and raw spuds.

Jeanie Quirt Brown

Sunday, April 29, 1945

Had first warm shower since we came here (lasted about five minutes). Had breakfast of porridge, stewed rhubarb and custard, bread, mayo and sugar, and Jerry coffee. No 0900 hours parade. Soviet Union Repatriation Board arrived last night, 15 officers, 20 girls and 200 other ranks with 100 tons of food in 50 USA trucks. Food included barley, peas, marg, 50 pigs, noodles, rice, etc. Already had enough rations on hand for 48 hours. They announced that since we were in an operational area, we would be moved either east or west, whichever way was open first, and we wouldn't be marching. It's a matter between the Ruskies and International Repatriation Board in Moscow.

Ruskies told of a camp near Lublin [Poland], where 11,000 people had been killed, mostly by gas, and their bodies cremated.[84] The ashes were used for road making and fertilizer.

Monday, April 30, 1945

Some of the boys have gone to a Hitler youth camp near here to prepare it for us to move there. Some Yank officers are moving this afternoon. Report says 18,000 more Jerry prisoners taken in this sector and fighting one-quarter mile from the camp.

Rations: one-sixth loaf, 100 grams sugar, raw spuds, cheese and marg.

Tuesday, May 1, 1945

Battle still raging close by. Bags of tanks, trucks and airplanes. 1,500 GIs and some of our officers and men left to clean up Hitler camp. Mussolini dead. Paddy out on scrounge—brought in 19 eggs, rhubarb, flour and fresh milk last night. Had three eggs for breakfast, bread and rhubarb jam, stewed rhubarb and custard and three cups coffee. Made

---

84 Majdanek was a Nazi concentration and extermination camp on the outskirts of Lublin, Poland, during the German occupation. The Nazis killed an estimated 78,000 people at the camp, although some reports suggest this number is much higher. Many also died of starvation and disease before the camp was liberated by the Soviet Union in July 1944.

custard of fresh egg, fresh milk, powdered milk, pudding powder and cornmeal and sugar, tastes pretty good.

Had one and a half cups of pea soup with about one pound of meat in it, and two cups of barley porridge. Ration of raw spuds but don't feel as if we needed them. Paddy, Harry Hargreaves, and Jock Lowry haven't come back.

***

Back in Napanee, Lorne's parents received the following from a New York State broadcaster. Unfortunately, it was not entirely accurate, as Lorne remained in camp awaiting permission to safely leave.

***

WSYR
Syracuse 2, N.Y.
Central New York Broadcasting Corporation

May 1, 1945

Mrs. Stuart Shetler
Napanee, Ontario

Dear Mrs. Shetler:
Stalag III-A at Luckenwalde was liberated by Russian troops early last week. I broadcast the liberation of Stalag III-A at the time.

Do not be discouraged if you do not hear from your son immediately, for experience shows that it is taking from three to four weeks for next of kin to receive direct news from liberated men or through the appropriate authorities.

I trust very earnestly that soon Lorne will be returned to you, safe and sound and with the abiding gratitude of all of us.

Sincerely yours,
H.R. Ekins

CHAPTER NINETEEN
Liberation
May 1945

Lorne's Log:

Wednesday, May 2, 1945

Didn't feel so hot, sour stomach and diarrhea, lay on sack most of morning. Paddy and boys came in with a wagonload of stuff—milk, honey, coffee, sugar, chicken, a goose, eggs, preserved pork, meatballs, jam, fruit, vegetables, and other stuff. They had met up with the Ruskies at a village where they were mopping up Jerries. They helped them celebrate May Day and insisted they stay all night. Ruskies found a wagon for them and loaded it up. They took wire cutters and made a road through the wire right into camp.

Thursday, May 3, 1945

Had a personnel check out in field at 1000 hours and then made rhubarb jam. Had two eggs, pork and bread fried in gravy for breakfast. For dinner at 1400 hours we had roast goose between three of us, masked spuds, diced fresh carrots, stuffing made with sage and onions and bread and honey, and black coffee with sugar. By far my best meal since a year ago Christmas on the squadron. There has been plenty of fighting near camp but mopping up in this area pretty well done now, practically no guns going at all. Streams of Ruskie tanks, trucks, Cossacks, wagons, tractors on road, about every man seems to have a tommy gun. French and other refugees wrecked Joe's place so GIs and advance party came back. They had horses, wagons, ponies, carts, everything. Horses are now selling for 20 cigs each. News good. Hitler and Mussolini dead and Jerries in Italy capitulated. Rumours galore of moving. Pancakes for tea. Announce over radio [Camp] III-A relieved. Wizard pancakes for supper.

Friday, May 4, 1945

Spareribs, eggs and fried bread for breakfast. Paddy brought some prunes, raisins and Klim so making pudding for supper. Lay around all morning, got up at 0900 hours. About one-quarter of the boys have gone off to the Yank bridgehead on their own hook.

A Yank colonel with a photographer and four jeeps came in afternoon. Had a rousing reception. Told us to be ready to move any time from now on with personal log and the clothes we stand in.

Report came in on the fighting around this district. 120,000 prisoners, 60,000 killed. There are supposed to be 10,000 dead in the woods just across the field from the camp.

Saturday, May 5, 1945

Still no sign of main body of trucks but 23 ambulances took out the sick from the lazarette.[85]

Sunday, May 6, 1945

Standing by for evacuation of whole camp. Twenty-five trucks came in the afternoon but Ruskies wouldn't allow them in camp. They went over there to load to Frankenforde and Yanks went out the back way but they finally stopped that. Trucks then went to Frankenforde and Yanks followed them. Most of them went that night and the rest went in a.m. SBO[86] announced evacuation postponed for three or four days.

---

85 Field hospital

86 Senior British Officer

Monday, May 7, 1945

Commandeered four bicycles and Paddy, two Aussies and I left around noon. Were shot at by a Ruskie leaving camp but got away and picked up Yank convoy beyond Frankenforde. Promptly threw away bicycles. Waited while they went on up road for more boys. Boys shot two deer in meantime and found Jerry rifles and stuff in the woods. When enough boys managed to get out of woods we set out, about 1,000 in 40 or 50 trucks. Liberated at last. After a few hours we crossed the Elbe, and those Yanks at the pontoon bridge really looked good. Arrived at nice receiving centre and given two blankets and then plenty more to sleep on, since there were no beds for all of us. Real chow coming up. Peaches, corn, chopped ham and egg, greens, biscuits. Strolled up to town but very quiet, curfew at six p.m. Canuck drowned trying to pull a Jerry out of the Elbe.

***

To: Mr. Stuart Shetler
Napanee, Ontario
Canada
(Undated)

From: F/O Shetler L.M. J86643
Ex-Kriegie Camp
Occupied Germany

Dear Folks:
It's a long time since I've attempted to write and I hope this gets through okay. I'm in very good health and not one of these physically wrecked prisoners that you read and hear about. After being liberated by the Russians and then re-liberated and moved by the Yanks, am now in a reception camp across the Elbe River. Am quite happy here and conditions are pretty good considering it's in what was the front line. Expect to leave here tomorrow for a camp where we leave for England by air in a very short time. Some of the boys are here and some are still in the hands of the Russians,

and rumour is that they may be repatriated by way of Russia and Odessa if the red tape ever gets unrolled.

How are you all coming along? Your last letter I got was written in November and you were all okay then. Since we were moved from Silesia to the camp near Berlin, I got no letters but got 300 cigs from Canada Brewers through the Overseas Tobacco League. The Yanks are doing everything they can for us here, and we couldn't ask for much more even if the war is over now. Well, I must close for now, hoping you're all okay. Will send a cable from England but you may get this first.

Love to all,
Lorne

***

Tuesday, May 8, 1945

Reveille at 5:30, breakfast at 6:30. Supposed to leave this morning. Hear 90 trucks went into camp yesterday and Ruskies doubled guard and wouldn't let them out. SBO resigned his post. Went up to town for shave. More boys came in from camp by way of Magdeburg. Couldn't get trucks across bridges so boys scrambled across narrow bridge and picked up by trucks on far side. US war correspondent there from Berlin trying to get across. Hadn't communicated with his paper in four days and didn't even know the war was over. Hear Hildesheim filled up and rations getting short here.

Wednesday, May 9, 1945

Still hanging around, really nice weather and beautiful spot here at Schonebeck at the Junkers[87] plant. Went up to town and bought bread, pickles, etc., with money and cigs. Issued K- and C-Rations[88] for noon. Expect to pull out tomorrow morning.

End of Log

---

87 A German airplane manufacturer.

88 K-Rations and C-Rations were types of rations issued to soldiers during the Second World War when they were on the move.

A Good Man

Lorne's last two weeks of log entries reflect, of course, his personal experience with the war coming to an end. He would have had very little detail of the significant events taking place on a wider scale at the same time, though rumours were flying.

On April 30, 1945, Adolph Hitler, seeing the writing on the wall, killed himself.

On May 5, 1945, the remaining German forces in the Northwest of Europe surrendered to the Allies.

May 8, 1945, known as Victory in Europe or VE Day, marked the formal acceptance of Germany's unconditional surrender to the Allies.

The Second World War was officially over in Europe and for Lorne. He was going home.

CHAPTER TWENTY
Repatriation
May–July 1945

Many years after the war had ended and the children were grown, Lorne and Ruth went to Disney World in Florida. Despite the ride breaking down, leaving them sitting still and listening to a never-ending loop of the theme song, "It's a Small World" was one of their favourite attractions. With that phrase repeating itself in his brain, Lorne would record his unlikely wartime experiences of meeting folks from back home while overseas and then former airmen and POWs once he was home.

This excerpt from his story, "It's a Small World," tells of his last day before being repatriated to England:

> *Two days later [after VE Day] the Yanks flew us, in Dakotas, to Brussels. No seats, but room for as many men as could fit on the floor. We were cleaned up and given new British Army uniforms and a little money. Another guy and I took off on our own and got lost. An American patrol car (MPs[89]) pulled up and a guy jumped out and says, "Who are you guys?" We told him and he looked at the other fellow and asked where he was from. "Prince Albert, Saskatchewan," he answered. He then looked at me and asked the same question. I said Ontario, and*

---

89 Military Police

then added Napanee. He grinned and said, "How are Mickey Dowling and all the boys?" It turned out that before joining up, he had been a delivery man for Coca Cola in my hometown area. Small world. He gave us some money and offered us a ride, but we couldn't take the ride because we were lost! However, we did eventually get back, with blistered heels. In the morning an RCAF squadron piled us in the back of another Dakota and we headed for England.

***

Canadian National Telegram via Western Union

May 19, 1945

RCAF Ottawa, Ontario

Stuart Shetler, Napanee, Ontario

Pleased to advise your son Flying Officer Lorne Melvin Shetler previously reported Prisoner of War has been liberated and arrived safely in the United Kingdom May thirteenth.

RCAF Casualties Officer

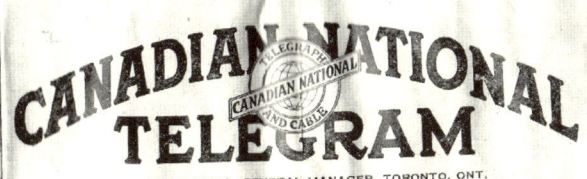

A Good Man

```
CANADIAN NATIONAL TELEGRAM
W. M. ARMSTRONG, GENERAL MANAGER, TORONTO, ONT.

R       S.      8.10 a.m.           30 Paid C.B. 2 ex wds

RCAF. Ottawa Ont.                   May 19th/1945

Stuart Shetler
Report Delivery,
R. R. 7,
Napanee, Ontario.

M9771 Pleased to advise your son Flying Officer Lorne Melvin Shetl
previously reported Prisoner of War has been liberated and arrived
safely in the United Kingdom May thirteenth

                    R. C. A. F. Casualties Officer
```

A photograph of the telegram advising the Shetlers of Lorne's safe return to England.

***

Royal Canadian Air Force
Chaplain Services

May 28, 1945[90]

Dear Mr. and Mrs. Shetler,
I was so happy to be able to welcome and chat with your son, J86643, F/O Lorne Melvin Shetler, on his safe arrival in England. He looks very well and is in excellent spirits.

Our boys are being well looked after by our people and it should not be long before they have "caught up" and are back to a more or less normal way of life.

---

90 One year, three days after Lorne was shot down

These have been anxious days and we join with you in giving thanks to God that they are ended and that Lorne will soon be arriving home.

Sincerely Yours,
S/Ldr. F.G. Ongley
C.12922 Chaplain (F)
RCAF Overseas

***

MARCONIGRAM
WORLD
WIDE
WIRELESS
CANADIAN MARCONI COMPANY

MRS STEWART SHETLER
NAPANEE ONT C/O Victor Shetler

JUST ARRIVED IN ENGLAND AND FEELING OK EXPECT TO BE HOME SOON GIVE MY LOVE TO EVERYBODY

LORNE SHETLER

A Good Man

> MARCONIGRAM — WORLD WIDE WIRELESS — CANADIAN MARCONI COMPANY (LIMITED LIABILITY)
>
> "Via Marconi"
>
> KI... VIA MAR SANS ORIGINE 14=
>
> NLT M... STEWART SHETLER
> NAPANEE ONT,...
>
> JUST ARRIVED IN ENGLAND FEELING OK EXPECT TO BE HOME SOON GIVE MY LOVE TO EVERYBODY,=
>
> : LORNE SHETLER,=

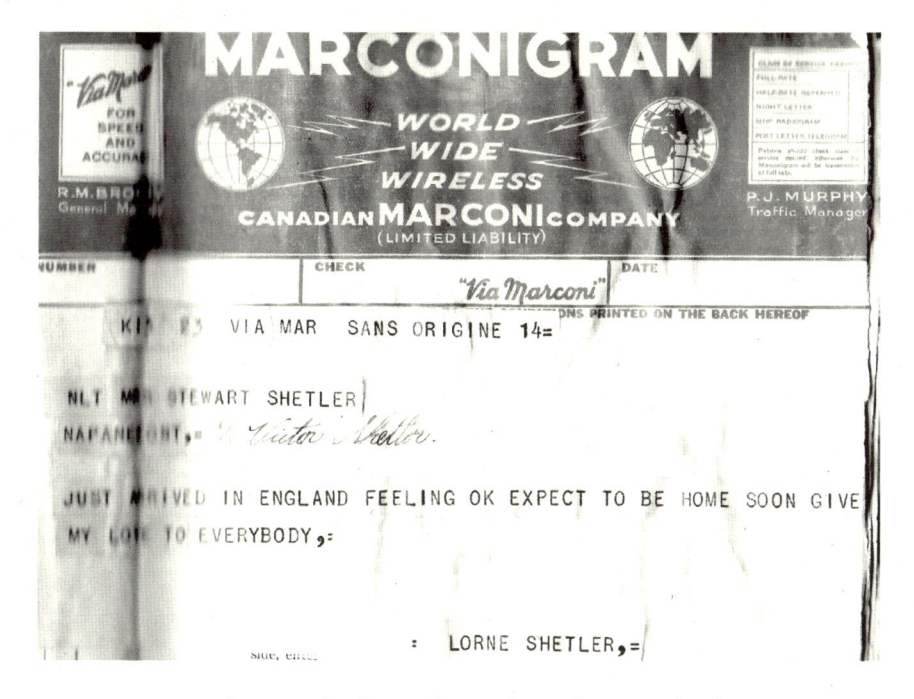

A photograph of Lorne's note home from England.

***

Bournemouth

June 4, 1945

Dear Folks:
Just came back from leave yesterday and today I found fifteen letters waiting for me, and was I ever glad to hear from you. These were the first I've had from you since last November and I'd been wondering how you were all coming along.

There was a boat that left the other day, but conditions were so bad that a lot of the boys refused to go on it and got off again. There should be another again the end of this week and I expect to be on it.

It's really swell to be back here again, and the people couldn't use us much better. I spent my leave in Edinburgh, Glasgow, Leeds, London and Bexley Heath, but really missed Ferdie, Bob and Mac. Still, there is nothing anybody can do about it.

While I was in London I stayed with Lord and Lady Chaplin and Lady Chesterfield, and they were swell. They said they wanted to entertain an ex-POW and I hope they weren't disappointed in me. They acted more or less like ordinary people and invited me back again…

***

Excerpt from Lorne's story "It's a Small World":

> *An ex-RCAF pilot bought a home on lower Simcoe Street,[91] and over the years we became close friends. One day he told me about flying a Dakota that was ferrying POWs across to England. Could I have possibly been on Jack Pearson's plane? I am not sure… but I do know it's a small world.*

***

In July 1945, after a prolonged leave in England, Lorne was among more than 1,000 former POWs and several thousand other RCAF personnel who arrived in Halifax harbour on the *Isle de France*.[92] The decks and rigging were crowded with jubilant men and women and the band played to welcome them home. From the ship they were escorted to waiting trains that would take them to their homes across Canada. Twenty-three trains left Halifax station that day—one every 27 minutes, according to the Halifax Gazette.

---

91 This was Lorne and Ruth's street in Napanee.

92 The 6th largest passenger ship in the world at the time, it was used to repatriate thousands of Canadian troops at the end of the war.

A Good Man

THE TROOPS COME HOME

As the Ile de France steamed toward Halifax laden with homecoming troops including more than 4,000 R.C.A.F. personnel she was greeted 180 miles off the Nova Scotia coast by a welcoming Hudson aircraft from the R.C.A.F. Station at Dartmouth. Thousands of men crowded the upper decks and rigging as the aircraft circled the ship for nearly an hour. This photograph was taken from the Hudson as the Ile de France cleaved through a calm sea under brilliant afternoon sun. The ship reached Halifax at midnight the same day (Friday, June 13). The repatriated airmen, including more than 1,000 former prisoners of war and about 2,000 volunteers for the Pacific theatre, were moved from the ship to special trains on Saturday and by late afternoon all were headed for their homes. —R.C.A.F. Photo

23 Trains, One Every 27 Minutes, Haul 10,000 Ile de France Arrivals

(Special to The Gazette.)

Halifax, July 15.—Twenty-three packed special trains, one of them bearing your son if he came home on the Ile de France, rolled westward bound out of Halifax's ocean terminals depot Saturday at an average rate of one every 27 minutes.

For days Pullmans and diners had been gathering in the railway yards at Halifax in preparation for this movement of nearly 10,000 Canadian troops. When the Ile de France came into the harbor, Friday night the huge ship was practically blacked out. About midnight, however, when she was warped into the pier, lights blazed on all over the vessel. decks were jammed with men and women of all three es catching their first of home after months or ars overseas. bands blared the pier, and a group of welcomers—all embarkals will allow on the pier to song to welcome the But loudest of all, even ian the bands, were the of happiness from the

swarming decks of the Ile de France.

Practically nobody on board ship slept Friday night. In all stages of dress and undress, they lined the rail of the ship, some just looking, others hoping to catch a glimpse of relatives, or even to get ashore and exchange a few words with them.

About 4 a.m., the first troops be-

Fog in Halifax Delays Hospital Ship Letitia

Halifax, July 15 — (P) — A thick fog which covered this area yesterday and today has delayed the arrival of the hospital ship Letitia, scheduled to arrive last night.

gan to disembark. They were a group of about 1,000 R.C.A.F. former prisoners of war, who w given top priority for disembartion. From that moment thing went with clock!

(Continued on Pa

A news clipping saved in Lorne's mother's papers.

127

Jeanie Quirt Brown

***

CANADIAN NATIONAL TELEGRAM
Montreal, Quebec

July 15, 1945

Mrs. Stuart Shetler
Napanee, Ontario

Just arrived Lachine should be home Wednesday or Thursday Love Lorne

F/O Shetler L.M.
J86643

***

When Lorne arrived back in Napanee, he popped over to his sister Helen's house to let her know he was back. As he walked into the kitchen without knocking, he startled her. She did not recognize her brother. His consistent weight as an adult was 200 pounds, but the man in front of her weighed less than 160.

Lorne with his parents and sister Hazel, date unknown.

A Good Man

Lorne reunited with Ruth Boston, left, and his sister Hazel, July 1945.

CHAPTER TWENTY-ONE
Letters from California Summer 1945

While the uncertainty had ended for the Shetler family with Lorne's return from overseas, many families were left wondering what had happened to their loved ones. There was no closure for those families, who were left with a void that would never be filled and a strong desire to know the details of their loved one's fate. The following is a letter from pilot Mario "Ferdie" Fernandez de Leon's mother to Lorne's mother Ethel.

Oakland, California

June 27, 1945

My dear friend,
I received a letter from the Dept. of National Defence for Air on June 18th. I will quote it:

> *"Dear Mrs. Fernandez de Leon,*
>
> *I have learned with deep regret that your son, Pilot Officer Mario Alfred Fernandez de Leon, is now for official purposes presumed to have died on Active Service Overseas on May 25th, 1944. I wish to offer you and the members of your family my sincere and heartfelt sympathy.*

It is most lamentable that a promising career should be thus terminated and I would like you to know that his loss is greatly deplored by all those with whom he was serving."

So you see, Mrs. Shetler, that I am still at a loss, not knowing what to make out of this situation. Such an uncertain time for me. We only know what you so kindly took such pains to tell me, for I know how painful it is to have to break news to a neighbour, friend or relative. The government presumes, they are in doubt themselves. I thought that by now they would have asked the crew that has been returned to England from Concentration Camps as to what or how it happened. But I suppose they attend to things in a different way.

I would like to ask you a great favour, Mrs. Shetler, a great service, for I know you do understand as a mother the agony I have gone through during thirteen months.

If and when Lorne gets back, which I hope very sincerely will be as soon as possible, will you ask him to write to me, and tell me with the utmost frankness if Mario was shot dead before he, Lorne, and the other boys parachuted, or if he was uninjured and just could not get out on time, or if he was completely and utterly destroyed in shreds by a bomb that may have hit the pilot's compartment. Assuming that this may have happened could be the only explanation why his body or his dog tags have not been found. Also, if Mario did confide in him some message for me, as boys often do in such cases.

Hoping that this will find you reunited with your dear son, and that I may soon hear from you.

Your grateful friend,
Amelia Fernandez de Leon

***

Lorne did write to Ferdie's mom on his return to Canada and was able to share with her what he knew. That must have been very difficult for him to relive as he too continued to mourn the loss of his crew mates. Mrs. Fernandez de Leon was grateful to hear from him and sent the following by return mail, as well as a letter to Lorne's mom who had supported her in the darkest days.

Oakland, California

July 28, 1945

Dear Lorne,
I have been earnestly hoping that you would return soon to your family, whom I can well imagine were eagerly awaiting to see you, and keep you with them for a long, long time.

I am very happy to know by your letter of the 22nd that your life was spared by Divine Providence, and although you must have suffered some rough treatment at the hands of the Germans, you were hopeful of being returned to your country sooner or later, and that hope gave you patience and strength to bear up whatever inconveniences and discomforts you had to put up with.

As you may have learned by my letter to your dear mother, we did not know of my dearest boy's tragic end until you wrote home and told them all about it, for the Government only presumed that Mario died in action overseas.

Then Helen Christie wrote and told me of Mac Stuart's cousin having gone to the graveyard, and was shown three graves by the caretaker. One of the graves was Mario's.

Yesterday I received your letter with the information I wanted to know, and although you could not tell me whether they were killed by the collision of the plane or because they were hit ... [illegible]... by the... fighter, you were unable to know the end, because God spared you the anguish of not being able to do anything for them.

So you see Lorne we have had to piece this tragedy together little by little, as ... [illegible]. Because to the contrary I had been informed[93]*...*

It has been a terrible and still an unbelievable loss. I cannot think of him as having left this world forever. I can only think that he was one who was not meant to return home, but to give his young life as others have done for the sake of Peace and Liberty.

---

93 The writing has faded and is illegible here, but she appears to be asking if the boys were killed in one blast and not slowly dying one by one.

I had come to know all the boys in his crew, he talked of all of you as if you were his family. He held all of you in great regard for he was a fine and sincere friend. He was meant for a better world. I cannot understand why he failed to have his dog tag on him. I thought the boys were not supposed to remove them at all.

Thank you Lorne for your nice letter and kind words of sympathy.

Please give my love to your mother, to whom I am very grateful for her letters of encouragement during these months of extreme sorrow and grief.

Sincerely yours,
Amelia Fernandez de Leon

***

August 20, 1945

Dear Mrs. Shetler,
I am enclosing Mrs. M. Cornelissen's letter that you so kindly forwarded to me in your letter of the 11th. Thanks a million. You have certainly been grand to me in these the darkest hours of my life.

Well, it happened the way I was very much afraid it would, and is always the case. They were burned. I hope they did not suffer any and they died instantly when it crashed.

It has been very hard to take and to accept this cross as part of my share of troubles and grief and desolation that all human beings are subject to sooner or later.

Yet, I am very thankful to almighty God that the plane did not fall into the sea but crashed near Tilburg, where those kindly people live. Besides they were buried in a Christian graveyard, in a separate grave side by side as they roomed next to each other when they were living and serving in the Air Force. I am also thankful and grateful that the other boys' lives were spared and have returned to their homes.

Thank you again dear Mrs. Shetler for all your kindness. Best regards from your devoted friend…[94]

---

[94] The second page of the letter is stuck to the pages of the book and is illegible.

CHAPTER TWENTY-TWO
Letters from Holland Summer 1945

It had been almost 14 months since the Cornelissens in Tilburg last saw Lorne, and they were anxious to know what had become of him after he left their home. The following letter was sent to Lorne's mom in July of 1945.[95]

July 13, 1945

A Cornelissen
Delmerweg 48
Tilburg Holland

Dear Mrs. Shetler
You should be astonished to receive a letter from a stranger in Holland, but last year on the 25th May 1944 the airplane from your son perished. So he arrived at my home in the morning of that day at 8 o'clock. We gave him civilian dress. We couldn't talk with him. We didn't know English at all. Now it would be better, [after] we have spent seven months with English soldiers. But we fetched a brother of my husband, he is a monk, and he could talk with your son. He spoke English and so we did our best to send him back to England. As we heard he was going there but we never more

---

95 I have made every effort to preserve the content of the original letters, but wherever English was not the first language of the writer, I have made minor alternations to spelling or grammar to make it more readable.

heard anything from your son because he has not our address. That was too dangerous. We got his address and now I will ask you how he is.

We don't have his military address, otherwise we should have written to himself. We are very curious how he is! His pals are buried nearby my home, they were burned. My husband goes sometimes to the churchyard. So, Mrs. Shetler, we hope to receive an answer from you. We are speaking often about your son and we promised him to write as soon as the war should be finished. If it is not too difficult, we would like to receive a little photo from him.

We have some souvenirs from him, his gloves and one glove with his name Shetler in it.

We fetched the next day some pieces of his burned airplane as souvenirs.

Awaiting a letter from you, we send you our kind regards.
A. Cornelissen

P.S. Please will you send us also the military address for your son. Thanks with anticipation,
A. Cornelissen

***

Letter from Mr. A. Cornelissen to Lorne:

October 8, 1945

Dear Friend,
We received your letter on 18 September and see you are home now. Sorry you have been in different camps in Germany. The people where you had to go to when you left us told us they were sure you would get back to England well and I thought it too therefore I did so. I'll tell you now the whole history since the moment you came to us and you'll see it was the best way.

A gentleman near to us brought you here. When you were coming in our gate he put you inside without saying anything, but looked at us to see what we said about it. My wife and I asked immediately "is parachutist?" He answered "Yes indeed. Should you dare to take care for him, for he has been by old man. He has slept there in the greenhouse and that man has two sons in the SS and three or four sons in the NSK (that means driver for the supply to the fronts). And he is a big chatterbox. I met the old man with him on the street, and if he says anything the Germans will kill us and I have seven children. Now I go to Breda by train for I want to have an alibi if anybody should betray us. So, if you dare, I leave him here."

I asked him, has anybody seen you. Yes, he said, one girl and that girl was very dangerous and four houses further lived two Landwachters (home guards), that are people who had to trace every person who was pro English. A son of those people was an officer in the SS. You see now it was more dangerous for you than you had thought. I asked that gentleman for a suit for you, for one of mine should have been too short. He immediately fetched one, and a hat of mine, and you were ready. Then I told him he had to go to the old man and he must say to him, he sent you into the woods, for he was afraid [to be charged with] treason. And he had to make the old man very afraid, and had to tell him not to talk to anyone about it, for otherwise the Germans would kill him in his own house and the old man knew that. Just some time ago six English pilots were shot. Members of the SD[96] in civilian [clothes] came in that house and without saying a word they shot those six pilots and when they were laying on the ground dying, they still shot at them. Worse than beasts. The walls were full of bullet holes and everything was soddened with blood.

After much trouble the gentleman went to the old man to tell him he sent you into the wood. He didn't like it because he promised the old man to take care of you. Then my wife went to my brother, that monk who has talked with you and he heard from you that you like most to go back to England. My brother asked you also, if you didn't know an address in Holland or Belgium where I could bring you. Sorry you didn't know anybody then. I would have been able to bring you there myself.

We had been also to the best secret organisation but because you like more to go back to England we wanted to try that first. We had called my brother from his school and another teacher told the children his mother had suddenly fallen ill and the children had to pray for her. So you see we were very careful. My brother couldn't stay longer. When you were in bed another monk came for the parachutist. But I didn't know him, and so I told him nothing to know about a parachutist etc., etc. But just on that

---

96 Short for *Sicherheitsdienst*, the intelligence agency of the SS and Nazi party.

moment a schoolboy came with two letters from my brother. One in Dutch and one in English for you. You read it in your bed, do you remember? Then I knew the monk was alright and he was allowed to go to you. He wanted to fetch you immediately before three o'clock. He told us you should be in England before next Sunday. My wife and I thought it too soon, we wanted to give you a good rest and to take care of you for some time. The person who brought you to me is a first lieutenant in the Dutch army, therefore he slept also in my home at night. Those two persons who were in the garden beside my house when I brought you away came also every night to us. They all had to hide themselves. So we should have hid you too. But that monk told us he was sure you should be in England by Sunday and the organisation was so very good that I could be quiet if you went with him. He told me also it was the best for you if I brought you away immediately.

I couldn't understand what he told you [in English]. If you write back, please write me what he told you when you were in bed at my home. My wife and I should have liked to nurse you longer but we thought also how happy you should be to be back in England soon and we thought of your leave in Canada. As you told us you would get leave when you got back from that raid. When I had brought you away, and had said you farewell, very coolly because I must be careful, I went again to that monk to ask him if he was sure everything should be all right, for when I came back home two gentlemen were here and they had already foodstuffs, carts and papers for you and they would bring you to another place, because Delmerweg was very dangerous. The monk assured me again that I could be quiet about you.

And so I am astonished to hear you have been in German prison. He was not allowed to say everything should be all right if he was not sure about it. I hope you'll write us now and then. If you know anything about that traitor, his name or his address, please will you write to us. My wife is a Belgian and she has a lot of acquaintances and family and we should like to find him.

Well Lorne I thank you for your letter and your nice photo. Has it been taken in Canada? It is just like a Dutch farmer's landscape. Please thank your mother for her letter and remember us to your brothers and sisters from my wife and me. My wife will write a letter to your mother today.

I received your letter. I have been to the churchyard where your comrades are buried. Now all Canadians have been carried to Bergen-op-Zoom[97] *and all Americans to Maastricht. But the crew of your bomber will still be there, for they were burned and their names unknown. On one cross is a name of a boy buried on the 25 May, 1944, maybe from your bomber, although that night more airplanes had been shot down. The address on that cross is from an Englishman:*

157590 Smith &
25-5-44
Smith F.E. J(?) Z.O.Z

Plenty Greetings from your Friends
A. Cornelissen
Delmerweg 48
Tilburg Holland

***

Letter from Mrs. Maria Cornelissen to Lorne's mother:

Tilburg, Holland 8.10.45

Dear Mrs. Shetler,
We were very pleased to get your kindly letter. We desired every day to hear from you. We were very glad to hear your nice son is alright. We were speaking about him often. Sorry he has been in prison. We thought it was sure that he was back in England. He will be glad that everything is good now. In the camp in Buchenwald where your son has been,[98] *many of our acquaintances were killed there. You ask me if we have suffered much in the war. Yes, it has been very fearful days and nights. We're living just between the main road and the railway, and they have been bombed and shot at very often.*

---

97 The Canadian war cemetery in Bergen-op-Zoom is home to 968 Canadian graves. There is an American military cemetery located outside Maastricht where 8301 US soldiers are buried.

98 Lorne had not been at Buchenwald; Cornelissen may have misunderstood when told he had been at Luckenwalde.

We have been refugees for three days for it was too bad and if we came back all was broken, there were no more windows, the doors were broken and all the tiles from the house, but it is fixed now a little. Just before we were liberated our windows were broken again through a flying bomb and now we can't get other ones. But that doesn't matter, we are no more afraid now. You can't understand what has happened here if you have not seen it. Every day it was something bad when the Germans were here and especially the last weeks. Those weeks I'll never more forget. We could write a whole book of it. Happy it is passed now. Maybe Lorne will remember. I asked my husband's brother to inform if the invasion should come soon and he answered, "Everything is ready for it," and every day we were waiting for it and it seems it was very long and now we are liberated.

Now it has to be some better with the foodstuffs, for that is not yet good. Meat we get just enough for one day a week and for three years we couldn't buy habits [clothing], also not underwear. With shoes it is just the same. So you understand what we have. We can never forgive the Nazis what they have done. I think it very nice to hear something about your household. My husband is a baker. Maybe Lorne has told you. We have no children. I hope Mrs. Shetler we'll meet each other sometime, you can never know. If you ever come to Holland you'll be welcome. Maybe you are living in your new home when you get my letter. We'll be very glad when we hear something from you again.

Many kind regards to the family Shetler from us both.

Yours sincerely,
M. Cornelissen

***

In the months after Lorne returned home, in addition to the letters from the Cornelissens, he received the following correspondence postmarked from the Netherlands. It seemed that Andre Group was trying to locate the servicemen whom they had helped through their underground organization. With the exposure of traitors in their pipeline, it was uncertain just how many of the airmen made it safely back to

England or how many were intercepted and turned in to the German Gestapo by the infiltrators.

AFWIKKELINGS – BUREAU
GROEP ANDRE
'S-GREVELDUIN-CAPELLE

Dear Sir.

There is about one year after you started with some boys of the "Group Andre" from Sprang-Capelle to the Belgian Frontier [to go] to Belgium and back to England.

You understand we all, Captain Andre and his boys, are very desirous to know what happened to you on your voyage to England, and if you really have arrived there. Therefore we should be very glad to hear something about you, especially if you arrived well in England, if you had still difficulties and so on; basically all that happened to you since you started from Sprang-Capelle.

As we have still some properties of several Allied pilots, we ask you to write us if there is still any of your properties in Sprang-Capelle and what they are. Please send us the address to which you want to be sent these properties and we will try to send them as soon as possible.

We have not addresses at all of some Allied pilots who have been in Sprang-Capelle. If perhaps you know something about them please send us their addresses, so we can write a letter to them too.

The names of these pilots are:
William D. Harris – birthday 10-5-24 No 11129380
Top Turret Gunner – B17 G
William Raymond Sheppari – birthday 26-5-25 No J 26349
Air Bomber – Lancaster
John Cecil Burns – birthday 6-11-16 No J 15830
Navigator – Halifax III
Mantle Alan – birthday 15-11-26 No 925315
Air Gunner – Lancaster W 890 J M D
We hope to hear anything about you as soon as possible.

With kind regards,
Yours truly,
Andre

CHAPTER TWENTY-THREE
It's a Small World

Once home, Lorne never expected he would again see the men with whom he had crossed paths during his training or time overseas. Canada is an enormous country, and these men came from different corners of every province. However, he was reminded by several chance encounters that it is indeed a small world.

***

Excerpt from Lorne's story "It's a Small World":

> *My future wife Ruth was in a Toronto factory during the war where they made plywood wings for Mosquito bombers. While on indefinite leave after I got home, one night Ruth and my sister Hazel and I took a night cruise to Niagara Falls. I had gotten paid and had about $400 in my pocket. We tried to go over to the US side and the customs guy asked how much money I had and I said $75. He said you have too much money with you. We turned around to go back and I was just about knocked down. And a guy says, "Tell him to go to hell." I turned around and there was Mac, the bomb aimer from Smitty's crew,[99] working for customs. When they were shot down, he*

---

99   Smith's crew were Lorne's neighbours at Leeming base. They were shot down and reported missing on their very first mission.

contacted the resistance and they helped him get across the Alps into Spain and back to England.

I never returned to the base at Leeming but when I later got home, I ran into our squadron bombing leader on a streetcar in Toronto; our wing commander at a pub in Kingston; and a fellow POW walking down a street in Weston.

CHAPTER TWENTY-FOUR
Napanee
1946–2005

As Lorne reflects on his time with RCAF, he marvels at how much of his life, and memories, were packed into those three and a half short years. It was quite a transition back to civilian life.

Ruth had been working as a carpenter in Malton, Ontario, building aircraft wings for Mosquito bombers, but had kept in touch with the Shetler family back in Napanee. With her carpentry skills no longer needed at the end of the war, she moved to a job with Employment Insurance in downtown Toronto, sharing a bedsit with her eldest sister, Elsie. Lorne's sister Hazel wrote to Ruth to let her know Lorne was on his way home. While on holidays in Napanee in the summer of 1945, the two were reunited and love was rekindled. At the end of June 1946, she resigned her job to come back to her family home in Hawley's Woods, just south of Napanee, to prepare for their upcoming wedding. Lorne and Ruth were wed August 3, 1946, and settled down in Napanee. One of the first letters of congratulations on their marriage came from Tilburg, Holland.

Till. 1/8/46

Dear Friend Lorne,
In your mother's letter we have seen that you have great plans.
I think it is very nice that you are getting married but you must promise me that you'll come here with your wife on your wedding trip.

We'll take care that you'll have no regrets about your staying here in Bergen-op-Zoom. I have made photos of the crosses on your killed friends' graves which we'll enclose in this letter.

Lorne, we wish you many happy things for the most important occasion in your life in the first week in August and hope you'll have much joy with your family on this day. Here in Tilburg, our thoughts are with you on this day and we hope you'll have many good years with your wife.

Well Lorne, please answer when you have some more time, and good luck and kind regards from my wife and myself.

A. Cornelissen
Delmerweg 48
Tilburg, Holland

Lorne Shetler married Ruth Boston on August 3, 1946, in a small church in the community of Morven, outside of Napanee.

***

Mr. and Mrs. Lorne Shetler would start their family one year later almost to the day, and over the following eight years they would bring four healthy girls into the world and build a family home on Simcoe Street in the west end of town.

Lorne was disappointed he never had a son. Maybe a little too obvious in that disappointment, as the doctor who delivered all four girls had to take him outside Ruth's hospital room for a talking-to, telling him he should be grateful to have four healthy children. And of course he was. He had also hoped one of the girls might be a redhead like Ruth. No such luck, but later he was blessed with two wonderful grandsons, Brad and Adam, and three smart, beautiful granddaughters, Amy, Jennifer and Jaclyn. He finally got his redheaded girl when Jaclyn was born.

After being discharged from the RCAF in the fall of 1945, he was hired by Veteran's Affairs, where his role was to help returning vets set up farming operations. After a few years he moved on to Napanee Flour and Feed, and then to the Department of Highways, where he was a maintenance foreman. Finally he settled in at Millhaven Fibres, where he remained employed until retirement in 1982.

He kept in touch with other crew and POWs who made it back from overseas and attended POW reunions in various cities and provinces. He and his former navigator, Ron Rudd, kept contact after the war and sometimes visited back and forth with their families. While the kids played and Marg and Ruth chatted, he and Ron would always come around to revisiting those days in May.

When they were reunited in Stalag III-A near the end of the war, Ron had relayed what had happened to him after he jumped from their aircraft. He had dropped headfirst from the plane with his parachute pack on his chest and the D-ring in his hand. But he had no recollection of the fall or the landing so assumed he was in a bad position when the chute opened and the impact had knocked him out. The first thing he remembered was hanging by his parachute from a tree, and then being unceremoniously dumped to the ground and dragged a short distance. He recounted he was in such pain that he didn't attempt to hide but just covered himself with the parachute and fell back to sleep. At dawn he awoke to see that he was directly below high-power transmission lines and was incredulous that he had missed them on his fall from the sky. He began to walk, and then, after a few hours of rest in a hay shed, he stumbled upon a German work party trying to put out a fire. He and Lorne later put two and two together and assumed the fire was a result of a fiery airplane crash. Perhaps theirs. He was, of course, detained by the German soldiers and taken to a prison near Tilburg.

Ron says he saw their wireless operator, Bert Dawson, there but neither acknowledged the other, as they had been instructed in their preparation for the flight missions. Bert would recount later that he had been picked up the same night by the Germans while walking along the road. They both ended up in Luft III, and it would be some time before Lorne was reunited with them.

Ron had been pretty good at keeping tabs on the boys, and Lorne inquired if he had any news of what happened to Dawson after the war. Ron heard that he stayed with the RAF but was then killed in an air accident in India a couple of years later.

Lorne never did make it overseas while the Cornelissens were alive. His daughter Barb visited the Netherlands after she finished university and she and her travelling companion were hosted by the couple. Despite the language barrier, it was obvious just how important that part of the past was to them. A couple of days in a lifetime for both Lorne and for them, but it was life changing for both parties. They were thrilled to meet his daughter. Lorne continued to correspond faithfully every Christmas but, as the Cornelissens had no children, the connection was severed when they passed.

While Lorne had been adamant that he had no desire to return to Europe, he and Ruth eventually did make the trip in June of 1989, visiting Holland, Belgium, Switzerland, France, and Germany. As Ruth recounted in her journal, it was an amazing experience. Lorne was able to pay his respects at the cemetery where some of his crewmates were interred.

A Good Man

The grave of Robert Christie, mid-upper gunner. The Cornelissen family took this photograph at Bergen-op-Zoom and mailed it to Lorne in August 1946.

A photograph of Mario (Ferdie) Fernandez de Leon's grave in Bergen-op-Zoom, also from the Cornelissen family.

Lorne and Ruth had a visit from Yvonne de Ridder Files, his Belgian helper, when she toured across Canada visiting airmen she had sheltered. They visited her as well when they travelled to Hollywood, California, where she had retired with her husband, a retired American Colonel.

Yvonne had been featured in a 1955 episode of "This is Your Life" hosted by Bert Parks, and several airmen were brought to Hollywood to recount their personal experiences of staying with her. Though Lorne was invited to participate, Ruth was heavily pregnant with their fourth child, Jeanie, and he was unable to attend. Charlie Shierlaw, however, did attend the filming, and fifty years later, after tapes could be released, he provided all of the Shetler family with copies of the show.

In 1991, Yvonne released her book, "The Quest for Freedom," relating her role in the Belgian underground and telling the story of her efforts to help many Canadian and American airmen. Lorne's story of betrayal was part of that book.

Lorne, much like other Second World War vets, never really liked to talk about what had gone on during his time overseas or in the POW camp. As he told one reporter who sought to record his story, "it's all water under the bridge." Perhaps it was just too difficult to revisit, or perhaps he knew that no one who hadn't been there could grasp what it was really like. For the most part, he only shared stories with men and women who had been there, such as Ron Rudd, Charlie Shierlaw, and Yvonne de Ridder.

With age, however, came a letting down of that guard and a window into his thoughts, and he did begin to share stories with family and those closest to him. It was always a very emotional and personal experience.

Lorne had a favourite saying that was reflective of the way he led his life after the war: "Can't get excited about it." He was calm and even-tempered. Nothing could rival what he had been through in the Second World War, and he did not seek out excitement but rather enjoyed his family and the simple pleasures in life.

The building lots in Napanee in the 1950s were very large by today's standards, and he and Ruth turned more than half of their back lawn on Simcoe Street into a vegetable garden with flower borders.

It provided the family, and not a few neighbours, with fresh produce in the summer and stocked their freezer and root cellar to tide them over through the winters. While most people might see caring for such a garden as a chore, tending it was a labour of love for them. And the fruits of their labour meant never again having to experience the hunger of the winter of 1945.

When the girls were young, the family would rent a cottage at Marble Lake and spent many happy hours swimming, fishing, card playing, and relaxing around a campfire. Day trips to the Sandbanks[100] in summer or playing a game of shinny on the frozen quarry in winter gave him great pleasure, as did Sunday afternoon drives.

Lorne did not envy others or ever live beyond his means. He and Ruth built their white frame, two story, four-bedroom home on Simcoe Street without ever borrowing a cent from the bank, and he would never buy a car until he had saved the cash to pay for it. It was a source of pride and yet caused him to be refused a credit card in later life, as he had never established a credit rating. He didn't get excited about being turned down because he didn't really believe in credit anyway; he was just trying to help his banker son-in-law earn points in a Mastercard promotion.

He and Ruth put three of their four daughters through Queen's University on one factory worker's salary. They were always most generous with their children and grandchildren. It saddened them when three of their daughters' marriages ended in divorce, but they did not judge and were always there to offer their support.

The years passed quickly and retirement brought with it increased opportunities for travel, golfing, fishing, gardening, and bridge. They volunteered with Meals on Wheels and at the Napanee Legion Branch 137. Ruth volunteered at the Lennox and Addington hospital gift shop and knit and donated countless baby sweater sets and mittens. Lorne promoted and supported the Red Cross at every opportunity, as he felt they had literally saved his life with their parcels.

---

100 A provincial park in Prince Edward County, Ontario, with beautiful white sand beaches.

In 1996, the girls gave Lorne and Ruth a wonderful 50th anniversary party. Yvonne de Ridder had been invited, but her health was failing and the trip from California would have been too arduous. However, to Lorne's delight, Charlie Shierlaw travelled from Ottawa to be there. This was a man with whom he had shared the most impactful and memorable time of his life, and the bond between them was apparent to all. In Jeanie's tribute to the couple at the gathering, she borrowed a phrase from her dad: "Be the good Lord willing and the creek don't rise," the family would all be here again to celebrate the couple's 60th. Sadly, they would only make it to 59 years of marriage.

Charlie Shierlaw with Lorne in August 1996, on the occasion of Lorne and Ruth's 50th wedding anniversary.

In May of 2000, a memorial to 429 Squadron, with the carving of a bison, was unveiled at the National Air Force Museum of Canada in

A Good Man

Trenton, Ontario. It was the highlight of a remembrance ceremony that paid tribute to the unit's service over more than half a century. Trenton had become the permanent home of the 429 (Bison) Squadron, and they were presented their colours. Lorne attended along with some family and was one of a handful of vets at the service. A dignitary speaking that day mentioned that three crews from 429 Squadron had been shot down in their Halifax IIIs on the night of May 24, 1944. Lorne was the only one present who knew the details firsthand, though his former wing commander, whose plane Lorne and his crew had crashed that fateful night, was also in attendance. Lorne assumed that after 56 years the commander had had enough time to forgive and forget. He and Ruth contributed to the project to restore a Halifax aircraft at the Trenton museum, and each have a stepping stone in the museum's memorial walkway.

Lorne at the 429 Squadron memorial at the National Air Force Museum of Canada in Trenton, May 2000.

CHAPTER TWENTY-FIVE
To Everything There Is a Season
September 2005

In mid-September 2005 Lorne sees his granddaughter Jennifer, who will be married next month. He can't make the trip to Toronto for the wedding, but it is nice to see her and offer congratulations. This is the day Lorne finally makes a much-longed-for trip to Jeanie and Nick's cottage on the lake. Logistics are tricky, but Jeanie is able to arrange multiple tanks of portable oxygen and a collapsible wheelchair for the outing.

It is a beautiful September day, though the leaves haven't yet begun to change, and he revels in being out in the fresh air and away from the retirement home. He follows his lunch of fresh fried bass and home fries with homemade wild blueberry pie, a favourite, and it is the very meal he has been craving. He feels content. He feels ready. He knows he won't be back again and tells Jeanie and Nick so. He thanks them for this day. Nick drives Lorne back to the home and sees him settled in his room. Lorne regales the staff with the minute details of his day, and they see the smile that has been missing for a while. When a caregiver comes to take him to the dining room for dinner, he insists he couldn't eat another bite. They tell him there is pie for dessert and he says, "well maybe just a little piece."

The next morning at 9 a.m. the phone rings at Jeanie's home. "This is Helen Henderson Care Centre. Your father is alive but unresponsive; should we call an ambulance?" No, she replies, keep him comfortable,

I am on my way. She knows he does not want another move, nor any interventions. He just wants to be with Ruth. The four Shetler girls gather at his bedside and keep vigil. Then, just 28 days after Ruth's passing, Lorne is gone. But his story will live on.

Lorne Melvin Shetler
March 1, 1917–September 14, 2005
He was a good man.

Acknowledgements

Writing this book was a labour of love and a deeply emotional experience. Spending so much time with my dad's writings helped me to understand more about the person he really was and how his early experiences shaped the father that I knew.

It was also a wonderful journey as so many people offered to help in so many different ways when they learned of my project. From old friends to new acquaintances, people were eager to offer information and pass on contacts. If I try to name everyone, I know I might overlook a name and I don't want to do that, so thank you to everyone who contributed in any way. I am touched by your generosity.

A special thank you to Sherry Baker Pringle of Napanee, an accomplished artist and author in her own right. When I shared my plans for this book with her, she immediately jumped in to encourage me and offered to design and paint a canvas to be used as a basis for my cover. What a wonderful gift.

Many thanks to my daughter-in-law Laurie for sharing her photography skills to duplicate the original canvas for print and for the author's picture.

And to my daughter Jennifer, who spent countless hours reading my manuscript and editing revision after revision, my gratitude and love. You gave generously of your time, which could have been spent with your young family and your own pursuits. It was a privilege to work with you on this project and I never could have completed it without you.

Appendix

Lorne's Crew

Pilot
Mario A. 'Ferdie' Fernandez
R143476
Buried at Bergen-op-Zoom, 5.G.12

Navigator
Ronald Beattie Rudd
J20248
POW #5505 at Luft III

Bomb Aimer
Lorne Melvin Shetler
R150081
Evaded, then captured.
POW #280 at Luft 7, then Luft III

Flight Engineer
William McGill 'Mac' Stewart
R50931
Buried at Bergen-op-Zoom, 5.H.9

Wireless Operator
Herbert 'Bert' Dawson
1515484
POW #78 at Luft 7 and Luft 1

Mid-Upper Gunner
Robert Foster Christie
R190930
Buried at Bergen-op-Zoom, 5.H.8

Rear Gunner
Kenneth Hawley Jackson
1239575
Buried at Runnymede

Printed in Canada